AMERICA'S U-BOATS

Studies in War, Society, and the Military

AMERICA'S U-BOATS

TERROR TROPHIES OF WORLD WAR I

CHRIS DUBBS

University of Nebraska Press • Lincoln & London

Library of Congress Cataloging-in-Publication Data
Dubbs, Chris.
America's U-boats: terror trophies of World War I / Chris Dubbs.
pages   cm.—(Studies in war, society, and the military)
Includes bibliographical references.
ISBN 978-0-8032-7166-1 (hbk.: alk. paper)—ISBN 978-0-8032-6946-0 (pdf)
ISBN 978-0-8032-6947-7 (epub)—ISBN 978-0-8032-6948-4 (mobi)
1. World War, 1914–1918—Naval operations—Submarine. 2. World War,
1914–1918—Prizes, etc. 3. Submarines (Ships)—United States—History—20th
century. 4. Submarines (Ships)—Germany—History—20th century.
5. World War, 1914–1918—Naval operations, American. 6. World War,
1914–1918—Naval operations, German. I. Title.
D591.D83 2014
940.4'51373—dc23
2014012340

Set in Minion Pro by Renni Johnson.

CONTENTS

ILLUSTRATIONS

ACKNOWLEDGMENTS

I am grateful to Tom Myers and David Myers, who planted the seed for this book by telling me that a World War I German submarine rested at the bottom of Lake Michigan. Like that wreck, so much of the story of America's U-boats lay unrecovered for over ninety years. To salvage it, I was assisted by many individuals and historical societies, each of which had some connection to the story of the surrendered submarines. Some were descendants of American crew members who served on the U-boats, some were passionate collectors of photographs and documents associated with the U-boats, and others were repositories of local history in which hid a long-ago visit from an alien, enemy submarine.

Numerous historical societies dug through their files to share with me their piece of the story. Indulgent friends and family helped during my research or in the final editing of the manuscript. Without their support, I could not have put together the mosaic of history found in *America's U-Boats: Terror Trophies of World War I*.

For their assistance along the way, a hearty thank you to Boston Public Library, Sue Turner Chapman, Mary Beth Earll, Diane Giles, Jacksonville Historical Society, Dwight Messimer, Don Nielson, Nova Scotia Archives, Craig O'Neill, Racine Heritage Museum, Rochester Museum & Science

Center, Sheboygan County Historical Research Center, Santa Barbara Historical Museum, Carolyn Fields Snider, Rusti Stover, and Deb West.

I am grateful to Frank Holowach, Innes McCartney, and Karen McKenna for casting their sharp editorial eyes over the final manuscript.

Special thanks to Gary Fabian for helping in many ways during my research on UB-88. Gary and his team were the first to locate the wreck of UB-88, and he now maintains the website UB88.org, an online repository of information on that surrendered U-boat. He gave generously of his time to help me locate resources and individuals connected to UB-88 and shared with me many of the UB-88 photos that appear in this book.

And thank you to Bridget Barry, my editor at the University of Nebraska Press, for believing in this project.

AMERICA'S U-BOATS

INTRODUCTION

In 1900 an attraction named *The Submarine Boat* opened at New York's Coney Island amusement park. The exterior resembled a battleship, bristling with turrets, protruding guns, lifeboats, and a deck. Inside, visitors could embark on a simulated submarine ride under the Atlantic Ocean and view through its portholes sharks, giant squid, and other wonders of the deep. The ride capitalized on the public's fascination with this new technology and the exciting possibility that submarines might soon make undersea travel a reality.

The 1904 World's Fair in St. Louis pushed the theme still further with the pavilion "Under and Over the Sea" that paired underwater travel with the novelty of flight. Fifty cents bought visitors a submarine ride under the Atlantic and the Seine River to Paris. Mechanical and electrical effects mimicked a submarine voyage, while views of fish, coral reefs, sea creatures, and shipwrecks completed the effect. After an elevator ride up a model of the Eiffel Tower (built for the 1900 World's Fair in Paris), travelers returned to St. Louis aboard a simulated airship.

At the beginning of the twentieth century, the concept of underwater travel still blurred the lines between science fiction and cutting-edge technology. The mere mention of the word "submarine" conjured up fanciful images of Jules

1. The *Submarine Boat* ride that opened at Coney Island amusement park in 1900 captured the public fascination with this marvelous invention. Library of Congress

Verne's wildly popular novel *Twenty Thousand Leagues Under the Sea*, published in 1870. The novel's Captain Nemo traveled the seven seas in the *Nautilus*, an underwater craft designed to explore and conduct research on the undiscovered world that lay beneath the ocean. However, the new technology also had a sinister side. Anti-hero Nemo had a grudge against oppressive governments, and the *Nautilus* had the ability to sink surface ships in pursuit of that agenda.

The navies of the world had already taken note of that capability. The U.S. Navy commissioned its first submarine in 1900. Other countries also acquired their first submarines at the beginning of the new century. In theory, during the period of massive naval buildup in which countries competed to build progressively larger and more expensive battleships, the submarine had the potential to level the naval playing field. Those countries without vast surface fleets now possessed a weapon that could compete for mastery of the seas.

In reality, however, prewar submarines were more a threat to their crews than to enemy ships. Mechanical failures doomed some submarine crews. The danger of noxious fumes from their gasoline engines or on board batteries prompted the Royal Navy to keep mice aboard submarines. The rodents served as canary-in-a-coal-mine sentinels to signal the buildup of deadly gases.

Writing in *A North Sea Diary: 1914–1918*, British naval officer Stephen King-Hall summarized the navy's bemused attitude toward early submarines:

> The average lieutenant, commander, or captain looked on submarines as dangerous craft into which light-hearted and nerveless officers descended and went out to the open sea, escorted by a ship flying a red flag; the submarine then dived and, after an uncertain period, rose again in an unexpected spot. Sometimes she never came up at all, and it was the general opinion in the Service that the submarine fellows fully deserved their extra six shillings a day.

That attitude carried into World War I, when the navies of the world saw submarines as novelties, with limited usefulness for scouting or coastal defense. But submarines could not match the speed of the fleet, and it was still Britain's massive Grand Fleet that controlled the seas, bottling up Germany's navy in its harbors and imposing a naval blockade on trade.

Attitudes toward the submarine changed dramatically in the opening months of the war when German submarines sank several British warships and later commenced their assault on the merchant shipping on which Britain depended. Germany's *Unterseeboots,* or "U-boats," achieved their greatest impact as "commerce raiders." Because German war strategists relied so heavily on U-boats to strangle British trade, they accelerated the development of their submarines, quickly evolving more effective and more lethal craft, far more advanced than those of the Allied powers.

Although U.S. public opinion largely supported the Allied cause, America struggled through two and a half years of neutrality, during which it officially favored neither side in the conflict.

Then, in the spring of 1915, one singular event fixed U-boats in the public imagination as objects of derision and barbarity. On May 7 a German submarine torpedoed the passenger ship *Lusitania*, resulting in the loss of 1,198 lives, 128 of them American. Even in a war prosecuted on a horrendous, industrial scale, with battles that routinely recorded casualties in the tens of thousands, this event put a new face on the inhumanity of war because it targeted innocent passengers, including women and children. The incident outraged the country and narrowed the divide between those intent on joining the war and those, including President Woodrow Wilson, committed to keeping the United States neutral. As U-boat attacks continued, with the further loss of American lives and ships, neutrality began to lose meaning.

By making several visits to American ports before U.S. entry into the war, U-boats demonstrated that they could operate effectively thousands of miles from their home base. The wide Atlantic Ocean no longer protected America from foreign enemies. A wave of books and movies imagined America's vulnerability to foreign invasion and played on that fear. Military leaders pushed through Congress a sweeping naval buildup to protect against such threats.

As a president thoroughly committed to peace, Woodrow Wilson struggled to keep a lid on the rage building in the country. But his appeals and ultimatums to Germany did not stop the U-boat attacks. Germany's declaration of unrestricted submarine warfare in January 1917, giving its submarines free rein to sink any ship in European waters, tipped U.S. public opinion toward war. When Wilson finally asked Congress for a declaration of war against Germany on April 2, 1917, he left no doubt as to what had driven him to that agonizing decision.

Vessels of every kind, whatever their flag, their character, their cargo, their destination, their errand, have been ruthlessly sent to the bottom without warning and without thought of help or mercy for those on board, the vessels of friendly neutrals along with those of belligerents. . . . The present German submarine warfare against commerce is a warfare against mankind.

Although Britain maintained a naval blockade of German ports, U-boats still found their way into the English Channel, the North Sea, the Atlantic Ocean and beyond to interdict British trade and the flow of war matériel. Virtually the entire focus of the naval war in World War I centered on the U-boat, one side working to perfect it and the other side to neutralize. The U-boat proved a dramatically effective weapon, especially when employed with the policy of unrestricted submarine warfare, a sink-without-warning strategy.

U-boats reached their zenith of development in 1918, just as the United States crowded the Atlantic with troop transports and freighters carrying war matériel to France. That year U-boats also attacked America, mining harbors and sinking ships off the East Coast.

Perhaps nothing better illustrates the novelty of the submarine as a weapon in this war than the fact that most of the naval officers and sailors who spent the entire war fighting U-boats never saw one; that was until the Surrender, when Germany's entire U-boat fleet fell into Allied hands and some submarines were distributed to the victorious nations.

Commissioned into the U.S. Navy and given American crews, six of the surrendered U-boats came to America in the spring of 1919 to begin a second life as war trophies. Their infamous reputations led the press to label them "Hun Devil Boats," "Sea Thugs," and "Baby Killers." Books and movies about the submarine war spilled over into that post-war summer as the navy took the vanquished U-boats on one incredible victory lap, visiting nearly every coastal city on the shores of the Atlantic, the Gulf of Mexico, and the Pacific, as well as cities along the Great Lakes. Finally, Americans could put a face on this diabolical mystery weapon that had nearly won the war. They lined up by the hundreds of thousands to tour the defeated enemy submarines, the popularity of which also helped to sell Victory Bonds and promote navy recruitment.

The U-boats also came under the scrutiny of the naval engineering bureaus and contractors that built American submarines. They thoroughly examined, tested, and dissected the U-boats so that their superior technology could be incorporated into the next generation of U.S. submarines.

Finally, as a provision of the armistice, all surrendered German naval vessels, including America's U-boats, were destroyed to prevent any nation from gaining a naval advantage by incorporating the former German submarines into their fleet. And yet, even as the U-boats were bombed, shelled, and scuttled to their watery graves, they served up one final benefit for the U.S. Navy.

1

THE FIRST U-BOATS IN AMERICA

The United States must be neutral in fact, as well as in
name, during these days that are to try men's souls. We must
be impartial in thought, as well as action, must put a curb
upon our sentiments, as well as upon every transaction that
might be construed as a preference of one party to
the struggle before another.

—President Woodrow Wilson, Declaration of Neutrality,
August 19, 1914

Rumor circulated in June 1916 that a German super-submarine was heading to America. According to the *Lloyd's Weekly News* correspondent in Spain, the submarine would arrive in New York, possibly carrying a letter from the German kaiser to President Wilson, asking him to mediate a peace. The submarine had left Germany a week earlier, or would leave in a week. The U-boat was seen at sea on a course for Boston, but then spotted at other locations along the coast. As conflicting, unconfirmed reports trickled in, newspapers struggled to get hold of the story and speculate about its implications. The very notion of having one of these menacing warships show up on this side of the Atlantic unsettled the long-held conviction that the wide ocean buffered America from the troubles of Europe.

The dizzying possibilities put the port collector of New York in a quandary. Through two years of European war, the United States had fiercely maintained its neutrality. As a neutral port, New York welcomed Allied and neutral ships by the dozens every day, but no German ship had visited since the start of hostilities and the implementation of Britain's crippling blockade of German ports. Rules clearly governed the visitation of belligerent warships to neutral ports, but one on a special mission, with a letter for the president? This was uncharted territory. He did not know what he would do if the boat arrived in New York Harbor. Would he order the boat to leave immediately or allow it to stay in port for twenty-four hours? Would it be entitled to provisions? Would he arrest the captain or take him to dinner?

On July 9, 1916, the rumor came true, but instead of surfacing in New York, the submarine appeared off the Virginia Capes. When a wireless message reached Baltimore that a U-boat had entered the Chesapeake Bay, newspaper reporters scrambled to be first on the scene. Converging on the waterfront, they hired whatever boats they could find to ferry them into the harbor. An incredible scoop had fallen into their laps—a chance to glimpse the mysterious weapon that had taken the United States to the brink of war in 1915 with the sinking of the *Lusitania*. Since then U-boats had further burnished their villainous reputation by sinking merchant ships, passenger liners, and even relief and hospital ships.

Twilight darkened the scene and a hard rain dampened enthusiasm, but the reporters kept their vigil until the submarine finally made port, escorted by the tugboat *Timmins*. Steamers at berth aimed their search lights in the visitor's direction, lifting its strange silhouette out of the twilight and illuminating the word "DEUTSCHLAND" on its stern. Though not the rumored seven hundred feet long, not even half that, the enormous, whale-like superstructure looked alien and sinister.

"Hello, *Deutschland*." An Associated Press reporter sailed close enough to shout questions.

"Hello," the captain yelled back from the conning tower. "What do you want?"

"Where do you come from and when?"

"June 23, Helgoland."

2. Tug boats escort the merchant U-boat *Deutschland* during
its visit to Baltimore in July 1916. Library of Congress

"Did you see any British or French ships?"

"None."

"Were you chased by any British or French ships near
the coast?"

"No."

That was all the news to be gathered on this night. As
Deutschland tied up at the quarantine station, the reporters rushed back to land to alert the world that for the first
time ever a German U-boat, the scourge of the seas, had
come to America on a mysterious voyage.

At 213 feet long, 30 feet wide, and 17 feet high, *Deutschland*
was the largest submarine in the German fleet. Throughout
the war Germany had developed its submarines from small
craft used for coastal defense to hearty boats that braved
the North Sea and Atlantic waters to strike at the commercial shipping vital to Britain's survival. The arrival of the
Deutschland in the United States demonstrated that Ger-

many had now developed U-boats robust enough to cross the Atlantic, a development that some in Washington and in the U.S. Navy viewed with alarm.

However, *Deutschland* represented yet another evolutionary step in the development of the submarine. The first of its kind, this U-boat was not a warship but a freighter, and its purpose was not to sink ships but to avoid them. By traveling at night and submerging when the need arose, the *Deutschland* had eluded the British naval blockade and made the first solo submarine crossing of the Atlantic.

The naval blockade was Britain's strategy for winning the war. In effect for two years, it cut the flow of raw materials and foodstuffs to Germany, suffocating the economy and crimping the war effort. The Royal Navy patrolled the North Sea and the English Channel, intercepting merchant vessels suspected of carrying contraband cargo to Germany or to neutral countries that might then transport it to Germany. Britain's extensive minefields forced neutral ships into British ports for inspection. Those ships without contraband would then be escorted through the North Sea mine fields.

The United States did not view kindly this interference with its trade. In December 1914, U.S. secretary of state William Jennings Bryan wrote to Walter Hines Page, U.S. ambassador to Great Britain, stipulating the likely consequences of continued interference with U.S. trade. "If it does not improve, it may arouse a feeling contrary to that which has so long existed between the American and British peoples." Even under these restrictions the United States, as a neutral country, continued to trade with the Allied and neutral nations, and would have gladly traded with Germany as well if only German ships could reach American ports.

A German shipping company headquartered in Bremen, North German Lloyd, thought it had the answer to the problem of the naval blockade: create a new type of vessel that could circumvent the British blockade and reopen trade with the United States—submersible freighters. While Britain's Grand Fleet interrupted all trade on the surface of the ocean, submarines operating like freighters would conduct their trade *beneath* the surface. After all, in the days before effective radar, sonar, and aircraft, submarines were virtually undetectable. The only way to locate a submarine was to make a visual sighting, and since submarines had such a low profile they were difficult to spot. Submarines usually sighted a surface ship long before they themselves were detected, in which case they simply submerged until the danger passed.

Because of their limited size and number, submersible freighters could hardly meet Germany's great need for trade, but they could bring in critical supplies and also boost national spirits at a time when they so sorely needed boosting. Lloyd built two merchant U-boats, *Deutschland* and *Bremen,* and at the time of *Deutschland*'s landing in America, had four more under construction. The reality of this venture was to be tested in Baltimore, where everything depended on how the United States received this vessel.

A Warm Welcome for the *Deutschland*

Despite a drenching rain, a crowd gathered the next morning at the Baltimore waterfront to catch a glimpse of the already famous submarine. *Deutschland* had tied up at the pier of the East Forwarding Company, the local shipping representative for North German Lloyd.

America preferred to keep its distance from European squabbles, a distance roughly equivalent to the width of the Atlantic Ocean. But the *Lusitania* tragedy and the carnage wrought by U-boats in the year since had tested American isolationism and neutrality to the limit. Scarcely a week went by without newspaper accounts of U-boats sinking merchant ships, passenger liners, and even hospital ships. Following increasingly strong protests by President Woodrow Wilson, Germany had finally halted unrestricted submarine warfare in May 1916, two months before *Deutschland* docked in Baltimore, in favor of "prize rules." Under this policy, U-boats had to first surface, stop a vessel to determine its cargo, and then remove the crew from harm's way before sinking the ship.

Now that one of the infamous U-boats had appeared in a U.S. port, people wanted to see it. To the great frustration of the public and the press who gathered at the East Forwarding Company office, however, catching a glimpse of the submarine proved all but impossible. A warehouse with a twelve-foot-high wooden fence topped with barbed wire extended the length of the pier, blocking any view of the *Deutschland*. When burly guards prevented would-be intruders from climbing the fence, the crowd moved to the far end of the warehouse where they could at least glimpse the bow of the exotic vessel and part of the conning tower.

A flotilla of sailboats, steam yachts, and rowboats cruised up the adjacent Patapsco River for a water approach to the U-boat, but they too were thwarted. The tugboat *Timmins* stood between the sightseers and the *Deutschland*. Those few boats that managed to slip past the tug encountered a floating log boom with a net that descended to the harbor floor keeping them at a distance of one hundred feet. A small barge with wooden panels at the stern of the U-boat further obstructed it from view. Two enterprising reporters climbed atop a pile driver scaffolding from which they kept a distant vigil for the next few days. The public hungered for any scrap of news about this extraordinary event.

The only person to have gotten aboard the U-boat was the doctor from the quarantine station who could barely contain his excitement. "I've never seen such a mass of machinery in my life," he gushed to reporters. "There seemed to be 5,000 different pieces, an inexplicable tangle of burnished

3. "An inexplicable tangle of burnished copper and glistening steel," was how one amazed visitor described the control room of the merchant U-boat *Deutschland. Collier's New Photographic History of the World's War* (New York: P. F. Collier and Son, 1918)

copper and glistening steel." His observations fed into the prevailing notion that this new German boat was a technical marvel.

Submarines of this period were primarily designed for coastal defense and short missions of a few hundred miles. U-boats tended to operate as close as possible to the British Isles, gathering in a few key locations off the coast of Ireland and in the Channel to await prey. But in two years of war, Germany had pushed the development of its U-boats in an attempt to counter the British blockade with its own interruption of British trade. Now, *Deutschland* had traveled four thousand miles from its home port of Bremen, through a naval blockade, and across the stormy Atlantic. Alone. No American submarine could have made that voyage.

4. *Deutschland* captain Paul König (*center*) on his arrival at
Baltimore in July 1916. Library of Congress

Later that morning reporters caught up with *Deutsch-land*'s captain Paul König when he presented his papers at the East Forwarding Company office. "What is there about my voyage to cause all this commotion?" König asked in fluent English, with only a hint of an accent. König and his British wife had lived in Winchester, England, before the war. He was fifty years old but looked older, as if his long career as a merchant marine officer had exposed him to enough sun and storm to etch a few extra years onto his face.

What he had accomplished would soon be common, he told reporters. Germany was building other large merchant submarines like the *Deutschland* that would maintain regular commercial service with the United States. In fact, one of them, the *Bremen*, would be arriving shortly. The British grip on German trade would soon be broken.

Although unused to the spotlight of the press, König

proved a quick study. He presented himself as a simple sea captain, his crew as experienced sailors, and blockade-running as a learned skill. He did not want their accomplishment to be seen as extraordinary. Extraordinary accomplishments were not easily repeated, whereas submarine trips to the United States were.

"What about the British destroyers?" asked a reporter.

"The North Sea and the Channel were as crowded with destroyers and as well-lit as Broadway," König explained, but the *Deutschland*'s sensitive microphones could detect the vibrations of ships. When one was detected, the submerged U-boat would stand still and quiet as a mouse, anchored fifty feet below the surface or resting on the sea floor. On those occasions "we drank good French champagne while we sang 'we've got rings on our fingers and bells on our toes,' and presently the destroyers gave us room on the roof and we came up and then went on to America. It was just as simple as that, I tell you."

Later that year, to capitalize on the publicity of the visit, König chronicled the rigors of his voyage in a hastily published book, *The Voyage of the Deutschland: The First Merchant Submarine*. It presented a more candid version of the dangers and discomforts that he and the crew faced on their voyage. Instead of champagne and singing on the channel floor, his submarine experienced an uncontrolled dive that buried its bow in the mud and projected its stern into the air. Fortunately for the crew there had been no prowling destroyers to take advantage of such an inviting target.

But aside from playing a deadly game of cat and mouse with British destroyers, the rigors of König's voyage to America resulted more from the boat and the weather than from the British blockade. In fact, unless the Royal Navy caught a U-boat on the surface, it could do precious little to stop a submarine. The depth charge had not yet been perfected.

Submarine nets and floating mines posed a risk in certain concentrated areas, but failing that, the preferred method of combating the menace was to find the U-boat on the surface and ram it before it could submerge.

Although König tended to minimize his accomplishment, the American public saw it differently. The *New York Times* labeled the U-boat's arrival as "an incident that compels admiration and stirs the imagination." An adaptation of Jules Verne's immensely popular 1870 novel *Twenty Thousand Leagues under the Sea* had just appeared in the movie theaters, and it was hard to overlook a comparison between the fictional Captain Nemo in his futuristic submarine *Nautilus* with the daring, real-life Captain König in his extraordinary undersea freighter.

Suddenly Verne's imaginative tale no longer seemed so futuristic. U-boats had already redefined the nature of naval warfare. Great Britain had maintained its mastery of the sea for the past century by investing in battle cruisers and super dreadnaught battleships. Nations had viewed the submarine as a novelty that had no serious role in naval strategy. But in the opening days of the war, the submarine U-9 electrified the navies of the world by sinking three British armored cruisers in the space of an hour before they were even aware of their attacker's presence. Now submarine crews sipped champagne on the ocean floor and provided underwater shipping service.

Under the terms of its neutrality, the United States was permitted to trade with any of the belligerent countries, but its trade with Germany, which stood at $345 million in the year before the war, had dropped to virtually zero due to the British blockade. At the same time, the United States reaped great profit supplying goods to the Allies, including armaments. The United States was eager to resume trade with Germany as well, but British dominance of the seas prevented that. The *Deutschland* and other submersible freighters might well resume the flow of goods to Germany, which was precisely what the British feared.

For several weeks in the summer of 1916, the main stage in the U-boat war, the clash of two imperial powers to choke the trade of its adversary, and the competition for the sympathies of the neutral United States shifted from the North Sea to the port of Baltimore.

Warship or Freighter?

Britain was quick to protest that *Deutschland*'s visit violated U.S. neutrality, a charge to which the United States was highly sensitive. Although most Americans favored the British cause in the war, America strongly resisted involvement. In an address to Congress at the outset of the war, President Wilson walked that tightrope.

> The people of the United States are drawn from many nations, and chiefly from the nations now at war. It is natural and inevitable that there should be the utmost variety of sympathy and desire among them with regard to the issues and circumstances of the conflict. Some will wish one nation, others another, to succeed in the momentous struggle.
>
> The United States must be neutral in fact, as well as in name, during these days that are to try men's souls. We must be impartial in thought, as well as action, must put a curb upon our sentiments, as well as upon every transaction that might be construed as a preference of one party to the struggle before another.

The wisdom of this position was amply supported by the grim statistics of the war. Scarcely a week prior to *Deutschland*'s arrival, Britain suffered a staggering sixty thousand dead and wounded in the opening day of the Battle of the Somme, while fighting at Verdun headed into its fifth month, taking its own fearful toll of death. And yet it was the comparatively miniscule loss of civilian lives in the submarine war that time after time drove the American public to outrage and nudged it closer to war. Woodrow Wilson's narrow reelection victory later that year using the slogan "He kept us out of the war" demonstrated the sharp divide over the country's continued neutrality.

In the case of *Deutschland*, the neutrality question came down to whether it was truly a merchant vessel, in which case it was free to engage in commerce, or merely a warship hauling cargo, in which case it was not. The Allied governments pressured the United States to declare *Deutschland* a vessel of war simply because it circumvented the law. According to international law at the time, merchant vessels could be stopped and searched and then sunk if they carried contraband. The Allies charged that since a merchant submarine could run submerged and thus avoid detection and control, submarines should be excluded from the rules of war that governed the treatment of merchant vessels.

On July 11, U.S. Navy officers gave the *Deutschland* a thorough inspection to determine whether it actually was an unarmed merchantman, as the German government insisted, or a disguised military vessel, as claimed by the British and French governments. At 213 feet, the *Deutschland* was close in length to a typical combat U-boat of the period. But whereas the combat vessel might be 20 feet wide and have a surface displacement of 650 tons, the *Deutschland* measured a hefty 29 feet in girth and displaced 1,575 tons. Like most U-boats, *Deutschland* had a double hull construction, with an interior pressure hull that housed the men and equipment that made the vessel function, and an outer hull. The double-hull construction provided additional storage space. Cargo could be stored both within its inner pressure hull and in the enormous space between the inner and outer hull. Because this space was open to the sea, it could carry only "wet" cargo that would not be harmed by exposure to salt water. However, on this occasion, the single most important difference between other U-boats and the *Deutschland* was that it carried no armament—no torpedoes and no deck gun.

The boat won the admiration of the inspecting officers for its size and the quality of its engineering. On the key issue of its status, they concluded that *Deutschland* was indeed a merchant vessel and could not "be converted to a war vessel without extensive alterations." This became the official position of the U.S. State Department and the Neutrality Board. *Deutschland* was plain and simple a merchant submarine, designed to thwart the British blockade, and as such would be welcomed in U.S. ports.

Opening Undersea Trade with Germany

The explanation drew loud protests from the Allied governments, but with its merchant status now established, *Deutschland* could set about its business. To guard against British spying and sabotage, the Eastern Forwarding Company worked in secrecy and adopted elaborate security measures. The company brought in African American stevedores from out of town to handle the cargo, making it less likely that the British could plant a spy among the group. Unloading and loading the submarine involved difficult and time-consuming work since the tons of cargo had to be carried through narrow hatches.

Deutschland had brought to America a high-value cargo of aniline dyes, medical drugs, and gemstones. Prior to the war, Germany had pioneered the development of synthetic dyes—known as aniline—from coal tar, and become the world's largest supplier. American manufacturers were eager to once again gain access to this source.

The cargo being loaded on board for the return trip to Germany included over seven hundred tons of nickel, rubber, and tin. The intended shipment of critical war matériel brought another round of protests from England and threats of "relentless reprisals" on every manufacturer, miner, and merchant that supplied cargo to the *Deutschland*. As a more direct means of thwarting *Deutschland*, Britain and France posted eight cruisers just outside the U.S. three-mile territorial waters, near the Virginia Capes, where the U-boat would have to emerge from the Chesapeake Bay.

But the concept of submersible freighters was too compelling and potentially profitable for Americans to side with the Allies. Inspired by the *Deutschland*, American submarine pioneer Simon Lake announced that he would build his own fleet of merchant submarines to operate an undersea shipping service to Germany. Meanwhile, the American public quickly embraced Captain König and his crew. Their exploits were celebrated at a succession of dinners, concerts, and tours, while newspaper coverage highlighted the technical accomplishments of the voyage and their warm-hearted reception. Captain König gave speeches and interviews, received awards and petitions of appreciation. Many people requested to travel as passengers aboard the *Deutschland* when it returned to Germany, though König politely declined these requests.

Baltimore mayor James Preston saw the commercial potential in reopening trade between his city and Germany. Preston hosted a dinner for Captain König, the German ambassador Count von Bernstorff, and a host of local officials, after which they visited the submarine. They emerged after an hour mopping their brows. It was plenty hot inside the *Deutschland*, they reported, and its huge diesel engines made a fearful racket, but it was a mechanical wonder. Among the amenities enjoyed by the crew were a phonograph and a library stocked with such American writers as Bret Harte and Mark Twain.

This publicity put a human face on the German crew. They were not bloodthirsty pirate Huns terrorizing the high seas as German submariners were often portrayed, but ingenious and daring merchant seamen. The well-spoken, affable König proved the right person to distance this commercial endeavor from the horrors of the war. His years living in England served him well in interviews and public appearances. In a sympathetic interview published in the *Boston Daily Globe* on July 23, König confessed that "among my German friends I am considered insultingly pro-British, and among my Ally acquaintances miserably pro-German." The war had done more to develop submarine technology than fifty years of peace, König suggested in the interview, but that technology now supported peaceful commerce. It was a swords-to-plowshares sentiment that resonated with Americans.

Lois Marshall, the wife of U.S. vice president Thomas Marshall, showed up with family members for a tour of the boat and emerged nearly speechless with amazement. "It's wonderful, marvelous," she told a *New York Times* reporter. "It is impossible for me to express my feeling." In the war for the sympathies of neutral America, such publicity was priceless, and it was just beginning.

Some of the *Deutschland* crew received a VIP visit to Washington DC. They toured the White House, and one of the sailors asked permission to sit in the president's chair in the cabinet room, which was granted. They showed special interest in the war maps hanging on the wall and pointed out their hometowns.

At the Navy Department the assistant secretary, Franklin Roosevelt, congratulated the crew members in German for their voyage. That night when the crew members attended a vaudeville performance at Keith's Theater, the stage manager called the German sailors down to the footlights. All Americans should be proud of these Teutonic heroes, he proclaimed, as the orchestra struck up the German patriotic anthem, "Die Wacht am Rhien," and the audience applauded for five minutes.

No one in Berlin, in the German war office, or in the German North Lloyd shipping company—and certainly no one in the British admiralty—imagined that *Deutschland* would be so well received. By any measure, the visit of the first U-boat to America had been a resounding success.

Cruisers Wait in Ambush

The high drama of the *Deutschland*'s visit would be rivaled by its departure. As it finished loading its return cargo, numerous rumors circulated about when and how it would make its escape. The British declared that they would sink the *Deutschland* on sight, and English and French cruisers waited in international waters off the mouth of the Chesapeake to carry out that threat. While the U.S. Navy maintained "neutrality patrols" to assure that none of the warships entered U.S. waters in their eagerness to intercept the German vessel, agents of the German shipping company visited Virginia ports to question incoming boat captains for information about the position of the Allied ships.

By late in the afternoon of August 1 preparations were complete. Crowds gathered on the pier to watch the sheltering log booms and barges being removed and the harbor entrance swept for mines. Reporters crowded aboard two large boats and followed *Deutschland* as the tug *Timmins*, a Coast Guard cutter, and a city police boat led the procession from the harbor.

A clamor of bells, whistles, and horns saluted the U-boat's passing. People lining the banks of the Patapsco River cheered and waved handkerchiefs. A huge convoy of small boats followed behind until the choppy waters of the bay forced them to turn back. Through the night, *Deutschland* and her escorts sailed down the bay, and then waited through most of the next day in a sheltered cove. The water off the Virginia Capes was too shallow for the

U-boat to run submerged, so *Deutschland* timed its exit for just before nightfall.

Only a large boat carrying correspondents for the *New York Times* and the Associated Press waited at the exit of the bay to witness *Deutschland* begin its homeward journey. They noticed that the U-boat had erected an odd structure on its deck to disguise its appearance. A high sea prevented the correspondents from rushing ashore with their news at Cape Henry, so they made for Norfolk instead. A full five hours passed before they could file their stories. By then they could only report that the *Deutschland* would have traveled some twenty-three miles beyond the three-mile limit and could be anywhere within a wide arc of the point from which they watched it disappear. Or it could have been destroyed by Allied warships.

In fact, *Deutschland* took twenty-three days to replicate its blockade-busting return voyage. Cheering crowds and ringing church bells saluted the boat as it sailed along the Wezer River on its approach to Bremen. Draped with roses from mast and conning tower, *Deutschland* docked at noon on August 25 after a round-trip journey of 8,450 miles. Bremen struck a medallion to commemorate the voyage. Germany was desperate for heroes at this point in the war and for some hope that the crippling hardships of the blockade might be over. *Deutschland* provided both.

Even as Germany feted Captain König and the *Deutschland* crew as national heroes, the U.S. Senate wrapped up debate on a Naval Appropriation Bill. The Great War had already given the United States ample proof of the need to protect its commercial shipping and prepare for such potential threats as a naval blockade and submarine warfare. *Deutschland*'s visit merely provided a timely demonstration of just how vulnerable the United States was to such threats. If a merchant submarine could come to America, so too could a combat submarine. If one could come, then dozens could appear. Virtually undetected, they could sink merchantmen and war ships, blockade harbors, and mine the shipping lanes. Passed on August 29, the appropriation bill committed the United States to develop a navy that was second to none. It called for the construction of sixty-seven new submarines, nine seagoing or fleet submarines and fifty-eight smaller coastal defense subs.

America's vulnerability to the U-boat threat would soon be demonstrated in most dramatic fashion.

A Combat U-Boat Pays a Visit

On the afternoon of October 7, 1916, a coast watcher at Newport, Rhode Island, trained his looking glass on two submarines heading past Brenton's Reef toward the harbor. American submarines came and went all the time from the naval base, and it was his business to recognize them on sight. He did recognize the first vessel flying the Stars and Stripes, as the U.S. submarine D-2. But the second boat was unlike any he had ever seen. He first thought it could be the merchant U-boat *Bremen*. He had been expecting the arrival of either the *Bremen* or a return visit from the *Deutschland*. But on closer examination he could make out the German naval flag flying from the vessel and a deck gun that clearly marked it as a warship rather than an undersea freighter.

A navy vessel in the outer harbor flashed an alert to the naval radio station, and from there word got out to the press. By the time the U-boat arrived in the harbor, a clutch of small boats were on hand to greet it.

When Rear Adm. Albert Gleaves, commander of the U.S. destroyer fleet, received word that a combat German U-boat had entered the harbor, he hurried onto the deck of his flag ship *Birmingham*. What he saw amazed him. The U-boat was huge by American standards, twice the length of the D-2 that escorted it. The designation U-53 marked its conning tower, and the German man-of-war flag fluttered from its mast. The U-boat appeared so clean, and its neatly uniformed crew walked the deck so nonchalantly, that it was hard to believe the boat had just completed the arduous passage across the Atlantic. The German submarine requested a berth and was soon anchored amid the thirty-seven naval vessels of the U.S. Atlantic Fleet.

The Newport correspondent for the *Boston Globe* was the first to scramble aboard at the invitation of the U-boat captain, Hans Rose. After a brief interview, Rose requested a favor of the reporter. "I have a letter here that I would like to have posted. Could I trouble you to take it ashore and drop it in the post office?" The letter was addressed to Count Johann Heinrich von Bernstorff, German ambassador to the United States. The reporter agreed to mail it.

International naval protocol for such occasions then unfolded with stiff formality. The U-boat was entirely within its rights to put in at an American port while on a cruise, even if that cruise was against the shipping of other nations. Under the law the submarine could remain in port for twenty-four hours, and if it needed repairs or supplies, it could remain long enough to make or receive them. Should a warship of the Allied powers enter Newport while the German submarine was there, it too could remain no more than twenty-four hours, and one or the other would be entitled to a fair start before the other would be allowed to leave.

A U.S. Navy launch arrived to take Captain Rose ashore to visit Rear Adm. Austin Knight, commander of the naval district. "Where is the submarine *Bremen*?" was the admiral's first question. The *Bremen*, *Deutschland*'s sister ship, had long been expected, but no one was yet ready to concede that she had been lost. Then the admiral proceeded with a brusque questioning to determine the captain's intentions.

"You want to repair your machinery here?"

"No, the machinery is in perfect order," replied Rose.

5. The crew of the U-53 when it paid an unexpected visit to the U.S. naval base at Newport RI in October 1916. Boston Public Library, Leslie Jones Collection

"Do you want to be interned here?"

"No, I will leave port before the time limit has expired."

"Then you come to land your sick and wounded?"

"No, my crew are all right."

"Do, you want fuel or provisions?"

"Thank you, I am well supplied."

"I see. What do you want here?"

"I came to pay you a visit, Admiral."

That tense, enigmatic exchange then shifted to a brief but more cordial visit with Admiral Gleaves aboard the *Birmingham*. In the meantime the U-boat was causing quite a stir in the harbor. Newport residents, including the Vanderbilts and other prominent families, flocked to the shore to find whatever vessel they could to carry them out to the strange visitor in their midst. Some rode aboard navy boats or loaded houseguests onto their yachts to visit the U-boat.

By the time a navy launch returned Captain Rose to his ship, he had trouble getting on board because of the crush of every type of vessel imaginable—yachts, motor boats, house boats, canoes, even rafts. When he climbed aboard, so too did a mass of spectators. The crew had brought a small phonograph on deck, giving the whole scene a lively party atmosphere. Then came the protocol of official return visits. First Admiral Knight came and went, and then Admiral Gleaves, who visited with his wife and daughter. They received a tour of the boat, and the daughter got to peer through the periscope.

Soon the lighthearted reception of a German warship proved too unsettling for the base commander. An insistent message arrived from Admiral Knight that all of the comings and goings from shore were to stop immediately. Capitan Rose got the message. He dismissed all visitors and weighed anchor. Within two and a half hours of its arrival, U-53 was under way, the crew lining the deck, saluting the American ships and waving their caps.

A launch carrying newspaper reporters escorted the U-boat from port. Two hours later, as U-53 once again passed off Brenton's Reef, the crew dismantled its wireless aerials in preparation for submerging and the submarine started off at full speed, leaving the press boat in its wake. A white light that had been shining brightly at its stern since sunset suddenly blinked out, and the reporters lost all trace of it in the darkness. It seemed a fitting conclusion to this mysterious visit, the U-boat disappearing as quickly and completely as it had materialized only hours ago.

Since the U-boat had braved the dangers of prowling Allied destroyers and mines and the harrowing Atlantic crossing simply to deliver a letter to the German ambassador, some reporters speculated that it was a harbinger of peace. Since regular communications with Germany had been disrupted, might this letter be instructions from the

German government to Ambassador Bernstorff to ask President Wilson to mediate peace talks?

Because the letter had been dutifully dropped into a postal box, reporters could only tell their readers the hard facts. They had pursued U-53 to the edge of U.S. territorial waters, at which point it passed out of the oasis of American neutrality and back into the war zone, where it became vulnerable to Allied warships and free to strike any ship it encountered. And, if it so intended, it could certainly find plenty of them only a few hours away in the shipping lanes to New York, busy with ammunition and supply ships.

"SOS Am Being Torpedoed"

Wireless distress calls of U-boat attacks began reaching Admiral Gleaves at Newport around noon the next day. Gleaves sent off his entire fleet of sixteen destroyers at top speed to the site of the attacks some one hundred miles away. Their mission was not to interfere with any further attacks, but only to assure that they happened in international waters and to rescue survivors.

U-53 had chosen its ambush spot well, at what was called the "elbow" in the transatlantic route where all vessels had to turn when making the passage to or from New York. Operating under prize rules, U-53 had been attacking ships since daylight, first a British and then a Norwegian freighter. The U-boat stopped the ships by firing shots across their bows, then ordered them to bring their papers to the U-boat so their ship and cargo could be identified. If they carried anything that could support the war effort (contraband), their crew was ordered to make a hasty exit aboard lifeboats before the U-boat sank their ship with torpedo, deck gun, or explosive charges planted on board.

By late afternoon when U.S. destroyers arrived on the scene, three ships had already gone down. The destroyers kept busy rescuing survivors while the U-boat continued its attacks. There developed a congested, chaotic scene of warships, sinking vessels, and lifeboats. As additional merchant vessels navigating these busy sea lanes continued to arrive on the scene, they found themselves caught in the bizarre panorama of a U-boat methodically reaping its harvest of ships while U.S. warships plucked the victims from lifeboats.

With U.S. destroyers as an audience, U-53 stopped the Dutch freighter *Bloomersdyk* and ordered the captain to deliver his papers. When U-53 determined that the *Bloomersdyk* carried contraband and would be sunk, it hoisted the flag signal for the crew to abandon ship. But before it could dispatch *Bloomersdyk*, the Canadian passenger liner *Stephano* appeared, and U-53 withdrew far enough to stop it with several warning shots. When U-53 turned back to the Dutch freighter, a U.S. destroyer had ventured too close and had to be instructed by U-53 with a signal lamp to move away so that the ship could be sunk. The destroyer promptly complied. It took two torpedoes to sink the Dutch ship.

Meanwhile, watching this drama unfold, the *Stephano* sent out a frantic wireless message, "SOS Am being torpedoed. American passengers," before putting passengers and crew into lifeboats. The *Stephano* proved an especially tough customer. Time bombs planted on the ship failed to sink it, as did some twenty shells from the deck gun. Finally, Rose used his last torpedo to finish the job.

At 10:30 p.m. Captain Rose and his crew ended a full and productive day. The U.S. destroyers headed back to Newport with 216 survivors, and U-53 began its voyage home, having disposed of five vessels and over twenty thousand tons of shipping.

Once again a German submarine had thrown the United States into a quandary. Had the action of the U-boat been legal? Had the United States responded appropriately? It seemed almost inconceivable that a solitary U-boat could operate at such a distance from its home base without support. This led to the suspicion that more U-boats might be prowling along the coast, or that a submarine tender lurked in the area to resupply and rearm such U-boats, or an even worse possibility, that the Germans had established a supply base in some isolated location on this side of the Atlantic—the Caribbean, Mexico, or the coast of Maine. The navy searched hundreds of miles of coastline but found no U-boat base, which suggested that these predators did not need supply bases to operate effectively thousands of miles from their home.

When the commotion died down, the United States was left with the troubling realization that the European war had now been transferred to its shores, making it far more vulnerable than it had ever imagined. U-53's visit left little doubt that if Germany chose to do so, it could effectively blockade U.S. posts with only a handful of submarines. The *New York Times* upped the ante with an article explaining how the entire U.S. battleship fleet could be sunk in a lightning U-boat raid. This raised the simmering submarine controversy to a whole new level.

On the same day that U-53 wreaked havoc on the shipping lanes off Nantucket, *Deutschland* departed Germany for a return journey to the United States. Two possible eventualities had been set on parallel paths. The *Deutschland* and her sister undersea freighters then under construction could conduct regular commerce with a neutral United States, thus easing the desperate economic straits in Germany caused by the British blockade. Or, more commerce-raiding U-boats could appear in the near future to disrupt American shipping. To a large extent the actions of U-53 had poisoned the waters and tilted the odds toward the second of those options. America's slow drift toward involvement in the war began to pick up speed. When the *Deutschland* arrived back in the United States, it met a very different reception than it had received in Baltimore.

Deutschland's Return

On November 1, 1916, *Deutschland* docked at New London, Connecticut. Arrangements for the submarine were similar to those in Baltimore—hidden from view, a fence and guards to keep away the curious. To the delight of the local business community, the North German Lloyd shipping company had built a new pier and warehouses in New London. New London mayor Ernest Rogers hosted a banquet for Captain König and crew, with two thousand people in attendance.

The European war was enormously profitable for American manufacturers, who could scarcely meet demand. But they had only tapped the Allied half of the market. A regularly scheduled shipping service to Germany on a fleet of merchant submarines operating out of New London had great appeal in the community. Although the German government now officially acknowledged the loss of the merchant U-boat *Bremen*, König stressed that other merchant submarines would soon be in service.

König, however, made the mistake of mentioning to the press that a combat U-boat might meet him off the coast to escort him home through the blockade. It was the absolute worst thing to say. Since König's second visit came less than one month after the attacks of U-53, outrage still hung in the air and the aftereffects still lingered. Insurance rates for shipping companies had risen sharply, and shipping schedules had been disrupted. No one wanted to see a repeat of the U-53 experience. Some speculated that the *Deutschland* had resupplied its combat U-boat escort with fuel and supplies before its arrival in New London. The mere possibility that *Deutschland* could serve as a support vessel for U-boats operating off the coast raised the anxiety level over this visit and revived the question of *Deutschland*'s status.

The U.S. Navy ordered a new inspection of the *Deutschland*. The enormously detailed report this time reached two conclusions that had not been raised after the Baltimore inspection. One, *Deutschland* could quickly be converted to a warship by simply mounting a gun on its deck. U-boats did not need torpedoes to function as commerce raiders. Also, it could easily be adapted to carry and launch mines. And two, without any alteration whatsoever, it could serve as a tender to several combat submarines operating off the U.S. coast. With its huge cargo capacity, it could carry spare parts and supplies. In its fuel and ballast tanks, it could carry reserves of fuel to extend the missions of the U-boats. Still embarrassed and angered from the U-53 incident, naval authorities would not be blindsided a second time.

A tragic accident during *Deutschland*'s departure further diminished any residual goodwill. While being escorted out of harbor, *Deutschland* collided with and sank a tugboat and had to return to port for repairs. Five crew members on the tug died. An investigation eventually cleared the U-boat of responsibility for the accident, but it nonetheless stoked bad feelings about the visit. This time, as *Deutschland* departed an American port, no cheering crowds sent it on its way and no boats filled with newsmen pursued it to capture a final glimpse of the exotic visitor. America had just witnessed the swan song of the merchant submarine.

The land war had taken a desperate turn for Germany, and its leaders had determined to use its most effective weapon, the U-boat, in a last attempt to strangle Great Britain's island fortress. One month after *Deutschland*'s visit to New London, the German navy commandeered the four merchant submarines then under construction and modified them to be long-range combat U-boats. The *Deutschland* would take on a new role and a new name as the commerce raider U-155, with the addition of torpedo tubes and two massive six-inch deck guns.

On February 1, 1917, Germany abandoned the use of prize rules in favor of a return to unrestricted submarine warfare. The impact was immediate and devastating. In January 1917, the month prior to this change in policy, U-boats sank 282,000 tons of British shipping. The first month after the start of the new policy, this number jumped to 464,000 tons. It would peak in April, when 354 ships fell victim to U-boats for a staggering loss of 834,594 tons of shipping.

The reinstituted policy proved the last straw for the United States, which declared war on Germany on April 6, 1917. U-boats would soon return to American waters on wartime missions.

2

THEY ARE HERE AT LAST

Admiralty informs me that information from reliable agents
states that a submarine of the Deutschland type left Germany
about nineteenth April to attack either American troop
transports or ships carrying materials from the States.

—U.S. Admiral William Sims, Dispatch to U.S. Navy Department,
May 1, 1918

In the desperate spring and summer of 1918, a year into U.S. involvement in the war, an observer might have concluded that America's role in the war was to put ships on the Atlantic Ocean. They would have been right. The small American fighting force in France had largely waited on the sidelines during a dismal 1917. But now the failed Nivelle offensive, disastrous casualties at Passchendaele, Austro-German victory at Caporetto, and a Russian-German peace treaty that freed up between twenty-five and thirty German divisions for the western front had suddenly raised the real prospect of a German victory before the United States would have sufficient forces in France to influence the outcome. A successful German spring offensive had the Allies calling urgently for a massive buildup of American troops as fast as it could be managed. General Pershing, commander of the American Expeditionary Force (AEF) asked for a million men. For American troops to save the day, they would have to arrive in France at a rate of at least 250,000 a month, and of course be supported with necessary armaments, food, and supplies. Could it be done?

The United States Shipping Board and Emergency Fleet Corporation had been engaged in the calculus of maritime transport since America entered the war. The Shipping Board had moved quickly to requisition all ships over 2,500 tons. It took charge of ship yards and began accelerated building programs. Through centralized management of all shipping, it kept the home front supplied, maintained shipping to Allied countries, and supported the few U.S. divisions in France.

Now the Shipping Board sharpened its pencils and did the math on General Pershing's request. The rule of thumb ran that for every man in the war zone, an army required fifty pounds of equipment and supplies. Multiplying that figure by 250,000 men a month would require a shipping capacity wildly beyond anything available. The rule of thumb got reduced to forty pounds per man, and then to thirty pounds per man. At one point, the calculations became so tight that it raised the real prospect that men could be delivered to the front who could not be fed. Additional shipping contracts were arranged with neutral and allied countries. Ships were called off the Great Lakes. Ships got reconfigured so they could carry double or triple the number of men. Every ton of cargo space on every available ship became critical. Only when the Shipping Board assured the War Department that it could support Pershing's request did the United States commit to the buildup.

The Atlantic suddenly became a much more crowded thoroughfare. Hundreds of individual ships still made the crossing on their own, but the men and matériel for the American Expeditionary Forces sailed in convoys of between five and forty ships that gathered at collection points off the U.S. coast and then proceeded eastward. Typically one cruiser and an armed merchant ship served as escort, until the convoy reached the dangerous submarine zone two hundred miles off the coast of France or Ireland. Here destroyers took over escort duties for the perilous conclusion of the voyage.

Britain and the United States had made significant progress with their antisubmarine measures. Still, U-boats continued to take a considerable toll on merchant shipping. Ships escorting convoys through submarine-infested waters followed a strict protocol that involved such procedures as zigzagging at full speed while the destroyers steamed along the perimeter. Any sign of a suspicious disturbance in the water would cause the entire convoy to make a hard turn while the destroyers rushed to the spot to drop depth charges, underwater bombs that could disable or destroy a submarine. If a ship got torpedoed, destroyers would render assistance while the convoy continued as though nothing had happened. To stop would invite further attacks. Trawlers with mine-nets swept the path ahead of the convoys and at the entrance to harbors. It was dangerous, expensive, and time-consuming, but these extreme measures minimized the effectiveness of the U-boats in the busy waters around Britain and France.

U-Boats Attack America

Simultaneous to the massive spring offensive of its army, Germany contrived a new U-boat strategy. It finished converting its large merchant submarines for military operations. Labeled U-cruisers, with a cruising range of twenty-five thousand miles and able to sustain missions of ninety days or more, these new submarines provided Germany with the capability of conducting sustained submarine operations well outside the confines of northern European waters. Some in the German command argued strongly against long-range missions. A U-boat operating off the British coast might log three missions in ninety days, so why send U-boats thousands of miles away when they could do more damage closer to their home base? But a successful 115 day mission by the U-155—the former merchant U-boat *Deutschland*—south of the Azores resulted in fifteen ships sunk, including an oil tanker and a British troop ship. Now that the United States had commenced vast shipments of men and matériel to join the land war in Europe, U-boats might have easier and richer hunting in American waters. Plus, targeting America might give the added benefit of drawing U.S. warships out of the European war zone. The war was about to come to America's doorstep.

On April 14, 1918, U-151 departed from its home port of Kiel on a mission to attack America. By this point in the war, life had become considerably more difficult for U-boats. In his book, *Last Days of the German Fleet*, German naval officer Ludwig Freiwald described just how suffocating the anti-submarine measures had become toward the end of the war.

> The channel barrier between Dover and Calais is finished. A barrier of beams, nets, contact-mines, listening apparatus, and yet more mines. Extending from the surface to the sea-bed. In triple rows of nets mines that can be exploded by electricity from the shore are laid at all levels. Besides these, patrol vessels of all sorts. By night, magnesium flares that light up the Channel as bright as day from shore to shore.

> But in the north the German submarines find their path blocked by a huge mine-belt extending from the Orkneys to Norway. The barrier of death. A vast American plan. One hundred thousand mines lurk there, like spiders in their web waiting for prey. At all levels American submarine mines containing four hundred and fifty pounds of explosives await U-boats approaching beneath the surface.

Despite these measures, U-boats still managed to escape from the North Sea and terrorize shipping. Following a perilous transit of the North Sea, U-151 set a course around

Scotland, south along the Irish coast, and then into the open Atlantic.

By 1918, the U-boat was a far more formidable weapon than it had been at the start of the war four years earlier. Because it depended so heavily on the U-boat, Germany's development of this weapon far outstripped the Allies. New models were larger, faster, and more lethal. Although originally designed as an unarmed merchant vessel, U-151 now boasted an impressive arsenal of torpedoes, mines, and two six-inch deck guns. At 213 feet in length and with a surface displacement of 1,700 tons, it was among the largest submarines in the German navy—in fact, the largest in the world. Newer U-cruiser models coming out of German shipyards were even larger.

During the month of May, a string of sightings and attacks plotted the U-151's course across the Atlantic. An American steamer reported the first sighting of the U.S.-bound submarine on May 2, 460 miles west of Britain. On May 14, U-151 made a failed torpedo attack on a British steamer about a thousand miles east of Cape Hatteras.

As the U-boat moved closer to the U.S. coast, the airwaves buzzed with SOSs and warning broadcasts as more ships sighted the enemy submarine or came under attack. The steamship *Nyanza* sent an SOS on May 19 after being shelled 300 miles off the Maryland coast. Shellfire set the SS *Jonancy* ablaze 150 miles offshore. On May 21, the British armed tanker *Cheyenne* exchanged gunfire with U-151 for two hours but managed to outrace the U-boat and make its escape into the Delaware River.

The frantic wireless warnings filling the airwaves did not initially raise a general alarm. False U-boat warnings had been common along the U.S. coast ever since America entered the war, even though no combat U-boat had operated in U.S. waters. Still, every merchant captain lived with the threat of sudden attack and with a chronic case of jittery nerves. Many a ship or convoy reported a suspicious silhouette on the horizon as a lurking U-boat. Ships would execute a sharp turn in mid-ocean because a ripple in the water suggested the wake of an approaching torpedo, or armed merchant ships would open fire on floating debris because it resembled a periscope or a surfacing U-boat. Through the wonder of wireless radio, reports of these U-boat "encounters" reached ship captains and coastal defense stations so frequently that they were often discounted. However, there seemed to be more substance to this latest rash of reports. The U.S. Navy knew very well what was happening and made preparations to meet the threat. But it could not yet issue a proper warning to shipping without revealing a vital secret of the war.

The unfolding saga of the U-boat attacks on the United States in the summer of 1918 played out in advance on the lined notebook pages of the radio intercept logbook in "Room 40" in the office of British Naval Intelligence. Week by week, sometimes day by day, radio intercepts were entered into the book. Because Britain had cracked the German naval code in 1914, it could identify with fair accuracy the location of particular U-boats and read the wireless messages coming from their base: Where to find the heaviest shipping traffic, lay mines, find a convoy route, or avoid bad weather.

Such information, shared freely with Adm. William Sims, head of U.S. naval forces operating out of Britain, allowed him to alert the Navy Department on May 15, 1918, that there appeared to be a reasonable probability that U-boats would arrive off the United States coast "at any time after May twentieth and that they will carry mines."

However, to guard the fact that Britain had cracked German naval communications, Admiral Sims stressed that it was "highly important that nothing whatever should be given out which would lead the enemy to even surmise that we have had any advance information concerning this submarine." This unfortunate advice put the U.S. Navy temporarily in league with its enemy. Whereas a prudent policy would have been to immediately alert shipping companies to the presence of a U-boat, Sims advised that whatever measures the Navy took should be done as secretly as possible. Therefore, the navy did not warn shipping interests of the approaching enemy submarine, and throughout the early days of the U-boat attack explained away sightings and sinkings with elaborate cover stories.

Three battered and abandoned schooners discovered at sea were towed to shore. Examination found that they had been attacked by bombs planted on board, a common method of sinking employed by U-boats wishing to conserve their torpedoes. The navy nonetheless claimed that the ships had collided. Alleged sightings of a German submarine in recent days were attributed to sightings of these wrecks or their debris, and the navy did not speculate about the complete disappearance of the crews from the three ships. For several days nothing more was heard from U-151.

Black Sunday

At 5:30 p.m. on Sunday, June 2, onshore wireless stations received a message that a ship had plucked fifty people from lifeboats off the New Jersey coast, survivors from various ships sunk by a submarine. Naval vessels rushed to the scene, and a warning immediately went out to all ships along the coast. The passenger liner *Carolina*, sailing sixty miles off Cape May, picked up a faint wireless message reporting that a nearby schooner had been sunk by a U-boat. The liner was bound for New York from Puerto Rico, carrying 335 passengers and crew.

The *Carolina* immediately changed course, assigned extra men to lookout, darkened its lights, and put on full steam for the nearest port. Unfortunately, the ship wandered directly into the path of U-151. The passengers, who had not been warned of the danger, were shocked when shellfire exploded the water near the ship. As passengers and crew took to the lifeboats, the radio operator sent the quick message "SOS Steamship *Carolina* being gunned by German submarine," but did not report the ship's position. When all the lifeboats got away, U-151 sank the ship with fire from its deck gun. *Carolina* had just become the sixth and final victim of U-151 on a day that would become known as Black Sunday.

Rescue ships worked throughout the night pulling survivors from scattered lifeboats as a storm kicked up heavy seas. Waves capsized one of the *Carolina* lifeboats, killing thirteen people, the first victims of German submarines operating off the U.S. coast. Lifeboats continued to wash ashore over the next few days along the Jersey and Delaware coasts, but nowhere more dramatically than in Atlantic City.

An early season crowd packed the popular New Jersey resort on June 4. A Shriners band parading on the boardwalk lent a carnival atmosphere to the day. The band had just struck up a lively tune when a ripple of shouts spread through the crowd on the beach. Lifeguards and bathers focused their attention on a small boat bobbing on the incoming surf. When it got closer, they realized that this was not a pleasure craft off course but a lifeboat in peril.

Men plunged into the water, including excited Shriners in full regalia, to pull the boat ashore. As men lifted exhausted women and children from the boat, the Shriners band broke into the "Star Spangled Banner," and thousands of onlookers cheered and threw their hats into the air.

The dazed and bedraggled survivors of the *Carolina* stared from newspaper photos like lost souls of the U-boat war. In the chaotic, unfolding narrative of the attacks, their stories wove into the confusion, misinformation, and desperate efforts to counter the threat. The public devoured

6. This William Allen Rogers cartoon depicts Gr. Adm. Alfred von Tirpitz, commander of the German Navy, as a pirate, bringing the U-boat war to the United States. *New York Herald*, Library of Congress, Historic American Newspapers Collection

each new detail of the attacks. Newspapers seized every rumor. Naval forces battled a phantom vessel that attacked and disappeared. One airplane pilot reported dropping bombs on bubbles, which he thought marked the spot where the U-boat had submerged. Lifeboats with bullet holes gave rise to the theory that the Germans were machine-gunning survivors. It later emerged that rescuers themselves had shot at the empty lifeboats to sink them and clear them from the sea.

As an interesting counterpoint to the attack stories, some survivors reported gentlemanly treatment by their U-boat captors. When U-151 began its attacks on May 25, it sank three small schooners and took all of their twenty-six crew members as prisoners aboard the submarine. This measure allowed the submarine to continue to operate in secrecy for a few more days. The prisoners went along for the ride while the U-boat planted its mines at the entrance to the Chesapeake and Delaware Bays, cut undersea cables off Fire Island, and attacked ships. Although living in cramped quarters, they were well treated. In fact, one of the captives, Capt. W. H. Davis, of the sunken *Jacob M Haskell*, later claimed that the U-boat's boarding officer Friedrich Körner "was so polite that it almost got on our nerves."

When U-151 commenced the attacks of Black Sunday, it no longer needed secrecy and so released its prisoners by adding them to the lifeboats of a ship it sent to the bottom. The Germans provided rations to the lifeboats and even handed over letters to be mailed to their relatives back in Germany. The captives parted on good terms with the German crew, a development that the polite Körner wanted to be widely known. In a post-war interview in Lowell Thomas's book *Raiders of the Deep*, Körner recalled the advice he gave when releasing his captives: "'You know the American newspaper reporters,' I said. 'You've got a big story, and they'll be after you in swarms. All we ask is that you tell them everything you know about us. Tell them how we captured you and how you lived on board.'" The prisoners assured him they would. Körner asked them to send clippings of the articles to him in care of the naval office in Berlin.

Today, at Last, the Hun Brings War to America's Shores

7. This ominous newspaper banner of German emperor Kaiser Wilhelm appeared the day after the "Black Sunday" attacks off the U.S. coast. *Tacoma Times*, Library of Congress, Historic American Newspapers Collection

Friendly U-boat officers aside, a headline in the *New York Evening Post* summed up the grim resignation with which many greeted the arrival of U-boats: "Well, they are here at last." Since the United States entered the war, more than eighty U.S. ships had been damaged or sunk by U-boats, but those losses had been in the war zone. Now U-boats had brought their piracy to America's shores.

Days of Panic

The day after Black Sunday proved one of the busiest days of the war for the naval bases along the Atlantic coast. As commercial ships continued to fill the airwaves with radio warnings and reports of rescued survivors, the navy scrambled to determine the exact scope of the attack and to find an effective response. Merchant ships hurried to the nearest port, and all port facilities shut down.

How many U-boats were operating off the coast? Where were they, and where would they strike next? Unfortunately, the United States had thousands of miles of coastline, and most of its destroyers and patrol boats were guarding the coasts of Britain and France three thousand miles away.

At Cape May, New Jersey, buglers hurried through the

town summoning navy men on leave back to their barracks. Observation balloons and seaplanes took to the air in search of the attacker. Aviators flew ceaseless patrols, locating drifting lifeboats, returning to base to refuel, and immediately taking back to the air. Submarines, patrol boats, and destroyers expanded the search up to seventy-five miles off the coast. Local residents crowded vantage points along the shore the first day after the attacks, reluctant even to return home when night fell for fear they would miss the battle at sea or a glimpse of a captured German submarine being escorted into port. Residents of Lewes, Delaware who heard continuing naval gunfire off the coast wondered if the U-boat had renewed its attacks or the navy had located the marauder.

In Washington, the secretary of the navy, Josephus Daniels, received a group of agitated reporters who peppered him with the questions on everyone's mind.

"How many boats have the Germans sent over?"

"Have you sunk the U-boat?"

"What is the navy doing to protect shipping?"

"Will you recall our destroyers from Europe?"

Our first priority is to "keep open the road to France, to protect troop ships and army supply vessels," Daniels insisted. "We are doing all we can to protect shipping and commerce, but the safety of troops must be our first thought."

Secretary Daniels and other officials downplayed the seriousness of the attacks, but the situation was already spinning out of control. Shipping companies, friends and relatives of crew members and passengers, newspapers, and anxious citizens besieged the department with over five thousand telegrams, radio messages, and phone calls on June 3.

Ever since U.S. entry into the war, it had been expected that U-boats would extend their campaign to America.

8. Josephus Daniels, secretary of the navy, hounded by
newspaper reporters. On June 3, 1919, the Navy Department
was besieged by reporters, phone calls, and telegrams from
people seeking news of the attacks and the fate of loved ones.
Library of Congress

Naval appropriation bills in 1916 and 1917 made extensive
provisions for coastal defense. "Defensive sea areas" established around harbors, ports, and bays created forbidden
zones between two and ten miles out, while naval aviation
fields built at strategic locations along the coast offered aerial patrol capability and quick response to threats at sea.
Because so many U.S. destroyers and sub chasers had been
sent to the European theater, the navy enlisted the help of
some five hundred private yachts and motor boats for antisubmarine patrol duties. Now the effectiveness of this defensive shield would be tested.

Various official measures were hastily thrown in place, but
part of the problem was that no one knew the exact nature of
the threat and how or where to confront it. Certainly ship-

ping was at risk. U.S. coastal waters now seemed as dangerous as those of the English Channel and the North Sea. Most major Atlantic ports remained closed for two days. Submarine nets sealed off harbors at night while spotlights swept the waters and patrol vessels guarded the entrance. All ships along the coast were ordered to black out their lights at night, and the navy hastily implemented convoying of coastal shipping and provided escort vessels.

But the U-boats also had large deck guns with which they could shell coastal cities, and speculation held too that they carried airplanes for that same purpose. In response New York City conducted air raid drills and dimmed its lights for two weeks to be a less conspicuous target. The city also thought it prudent to mount anti-aircraft guns on the Hudson River Palisades. In Boston, the gold dome on the Massachusetts State House got a quick coat of gray paint to camouflage it from air attack.

These practical measures were set within the context of the public's paranoid speculation about how such a terrible thing could happen. Stories circulated that U-boats had secret bases in Mexico, as did a host of other rumors and misinformation: The U-boat had incendiary shells to lob onto New York City and germs to spray on New Jersey. The naval commandant at Norfolk confirmed an erroneous report that *five* U-boats were operating off the Virginia coast. That gave rise to a rumor that Paul König, the affable captain of the merchant submarine *Deutschland*, had returned with a pack of U-boats to terrorize the country that had so warmly embraced him.

Rumor spread that the U-boat had landed spies at Cape May and that wireless stations hidden in the pine woods of New Jersey transmitted information to German submarines offshore. This appeared to lend credence to the suspicion of German-Americans that had flourished since the United States entered the war. New York City police raided

German clubs that had shown too much satisfaction at the exploits of the U-boat. Some German-Americans were denounced or arrested. The conviction had formed that something unique to the German character explained the inhumane way that Germany conducted the war, especially the submarine war.

In the book *The Martial Adventures of Henry and Me*, published just one month prior to Black Sunday, legendary newspaper editor, politician, and author William Allen White told the story of a fictional newspaper editor from Wichita sent to the war zone to investigate the Red Cross. He takes with him a provincial attitude about the wider world, but an attitude that could neatly distill complex issues down to the simplest terms.

On the voyage to Europe his ship gets a distress call from another vessel and, to his astonishment, it speeds away as fast as possible. The explanation he receives is that such distress signals are a favorite U-boat trick to lure ships into an ambush. "I've been thinking about this U-boat business, how it would be if we had the German's job," the editor is moved to reflect.

> I have been trying to think if there is anyone in Wichita who could go out and run a U-boat the way these Germans run U-boats, and I've been trying to imagine him sitting on the front porch of the Country Club or down at the Elks Club talking about it; telling how he lured the Captain of a ship by his distress signals to come to the rescue of a sinking ship and then destroyed the rescuer, and I've been trying to figure out how the fellows sitting around him would take it. They'd get up and leave. He'd be outcast as unspeakable, and no brag or bluff or blare of victory would gloss over his act. We simply don't think the German way. We have a loyalty to humanity deeper than patriotism. There are certain things that self-respecting

men can't do and live in Wichita. But there seems to be no restrictions in Germany.

Through his widely reprinted editorials, White had built a national reputation as the iconic spokesman for the middle class. His simple and poignant anecdote better captured the attitude that had seized Americans than did any of the political, military, or philosophical rationales put forth. It tapped the vein of outrage from the *Lusitania*, anger at the relentless attacks on merchant ships, and the revulsion felt when passenger and hospital ships fell victim to the U-boat assault.

The musings of White's fictional editor neatly illustrated what had emerged as the central theme of the conflict, that the war was a clash between free Western democracies that subscribed to basic human values and an autocratic Germany in which all values were subordinated to the interests of the state. Attacks against shipping were portrayed as attacks against civilization.

Now that such fictions had turned frighteningly real, a surge of patriotism drove young men to recruiting stations in record numbers. The day after Black Sunday, additional recruiting offices had to be opened in San Francisco, while in New York would-be recruits began lining up at six o'clock in the morning. The line at the East 23rd Street recruiting station extended from its office on the third floor down three flights of stairs and a block along the street outside. "U-boat Visit has Awakened America," announced a *Boston Daily Globe* headline. "This U-boat attack is the best thing that has happened to America," the article claimed, "for it has compelled Americans to realize that we are actually at war."

There was a grim logic in that claim. American doughboys were only now heading to the war by the hundreds of thousands, and casualty lists had not yet started appearing in the newspapers. Other than repeated bond drives to pay for military buildup and operations, Americans paid little price for their first year of involvement in World War I. The war had stayed conveniently "over there." In fact the war had lifted the country out of a depression as a huge trade in war materials spurred growth in the economy. Industry boomed. Wages soared. Food was abundant. Theaters were packed. Pleasure automobile sales rose over the previous year. Now, it appeared as though the bill for this bountiful isolation had finally come due.

The appearance of U-151 renewed the controversy about the American policy of deploying its naval assets to Europe. During the first year of the war, the United States sent most of its newly-built destroyers and submarine chasers to fight U-boats in European waters. Since no U-boats had appeared in U.S. waters in 1917, it made sense to concentrate naval might in the active war zones of the North Sea, English Channel, and British and French coastal waters rather than have them patrolling the peaceful, sprawling vastness of America's Atlantic coast.

But as sinkings continued in the weeks and months after June 2, growing frustration and anger focused squarely on the navy. Navy vessels and airplanes maintained constant patrols, but finding a solitary submarine along three thousand miles of coast proved a hopeless task. Plus, danger lingered in an area even after the U-boat departed. On June 3 the oil tanker *Herbert L. Pratt* struck a mine and sank in the Delaware Bay en route to Philadelphia. Minesweepers immediately cleared the channel and also located and cleared mines laid in the mouth of the Chesapeake.

The navy took control of coastal shipping, issuing orders for the movement of all ships. Convoys ran in daylight hours, escorted by a ragtag mix of warships, converted yachts and trawlers, and some of the new sub chasers. A "hunt squadron" of six sub chasers, a destroyer, flying boats,

9. U-boats sank ships off the U.S. coast in 1918 using prize
rules. Here popular German artist Willy Stöwer captures
such an encounter between a U-boat and a freighter. After the
captain brings his papers to the U-boat and the crew takes to
the lifeboats, the ship would be sunk.

and blimps patrolled out of Norfolk. Twelve naval aviation
patrols units continually scoured coastal waters without
sighting the elusive enemy.

Critics pointed out the irony of the current situation.
Despite having passed the mammoth Naval Bill in 1916
that promised to build the greatest navy in the world, the
United States was now being held hostage by a solitary submarine. Calls for a congressional investigation never gained
traction, as public figures made statements in support of
the navy and its tactics. In an effort to further strengthen
coastal defense, Congress appropriated funding for sixteen
new balloon and airplane stations along the Atlantic coast.

Although most ships had found shelter in the nearest
port or traveled in safety as part of coastal convoys, U-151
continued to find victims in the weeks after Black Sunday.
The U-boat took an especially rich prize when it stopped
the Norwegian freighter *Vindeggen*, which carried a load

of copper, a critical war material in short supply in Germany. While in the process of transferring eighty tons of ingots to the U-boat, U-151 had to pause to sink another ship that happened by. The submarine later forced a third ship to stop and pick up the survivors of the first two ships and take them to port.

Ships continued to report U-boat sightings, even after U-151 left behind its rich harvest in U.S. waters to return to its base in Kiel. Its mission had been an unqualified success, having covered over 10,000 miles in about 30 days. In that time the U-boat sank 23 ships weighing a total of 58,028 tons, planted two mine fields in well-traveled shipping lanes, cut two undersea cables, and returned to Germany with a load of precious copper. And unlike U-boat missions in European waters, it had encountered virtually no resistance. U-151 took back to its base the message that the U.S. coast was essentially undefended.

A second U-boat, U-156, another converted merchant submarine, was already on its way to the United States to take up where U-151 had left off. Others would follow throughout the summer.

3

FIGHTING THE U-BOATS

*Today one of the impressive Fourth of July celebrations
will be the launching of fourteen new destroyers, and scores
more will be launched and commissioned before the end of
the summer, with an increasing number thereafter until
these best foes of the submarines . . . free the world
forever of the assassins of the seas.*

—Secretary of the Navy Josephus Daniels, *New York Tribune,*
July 4, 1918

The *Boston Globe* reporter taking the phone call from Dr.
Joshua Danforth Taylor on July 21, 1918, must have been
more than a little incredulous. No one had ever before
called the newspaper to report that the U.S. mainland was
under enemy attack. But that was precisely what Dr. Taylor
claimed. A German submarine had surfaced in an oceanside
estuary of the Cape Cod peninsula, near the quiet town of
Orleans, and commenced attacking shipping and lobbing
shells onto land. Standing outside his summer cottage on
Nauset Bluffs, Dr. Taylor gave the *Globe* a world exclusive,
blow-by-blow description of the attack.

Distant explosions first alerted Orleans residents and summer tourists to the unfolding events. The rumbling reminded
many of the Atlantic Fleet's prewar target practice in Cape
Cod Bay. Dr. Taylor knew otherwise. From the bluffs he
could see a tugboat and several barges near the Nauset Inlet,
and on the surface not far away sat a submarine firing its
deck gun. The sub scored three quick hits on the tug. Pan-
icky bathers nearby out for a morning dip scurried ashore. As
the U-boat turned its fury on the three barges that had been
in tow, Danforth continued his commentary to the *Globe*.

Prior to U.S. entry into the war, a type of fiction, now called "invasion literature," fed paranoia about America's unpreparedness for war. Books such as *Defenseless America* (1915), *America Fallen* (1915), *The Conquest of America* (1915), and *A Fall of a Nation* (1916) raised the specter of a German invasion. The assistant secretary of the navy, Franklin Roosevelt, had foreseen the possibility of such an unlikely attack. In 1917, shortly after the United States entered the war, he wrote to his wife, Eleanor, then at their summer home in Maine, "I meant to tell you, if by any perfectly wild chance a German submarine should come into the bay and start to shell Eastport or the Pool [Welshpool], I want you to grab the children and beat it into the woods."

Now the whole incredible invasion scenario seemed to be playing out in quiet Nauset Bay. The booming reverberation of the gunfire caught the attention of personnel at the nearby Coast Guard station, who rushed to their lookout tower in time to witness shells exploding on the tug and the crew taking to lifeboats. The tug boat was ablaze. The Coast Guard observers could clearly see the gray hull of the U-boat riding low in the water, and on deck, groups of men clustered around the fore and aft deck guns, firing at the barges.

The station placed a frantic phone call to the nearby Chatham Naval Air Station, where officers were at first incredulous. A German submarine in Nauset Bay? Attacking a tug boat? There had been so many false reports; it was hard to know how much credence to give this phone call. However, U-boats were known to be operating off the coast. That very morning the paper reported the sinking of the armored cruiser USS *San Diego*, which had been sailing off Long Island, headed for New York to escort a convoy. Sixty-two members of its crew were still missing. The *San Diego* may have been the victim of one of the seven U-boats then thought to be operating in American waters, or it may have struck a submarine-laid mine. Though the Chatham

Air Station had only a skeleton crew on duty that day, it hastily armed four planes with bombs and sent them off to strike the U-boat.

The citizens of Orleans gathered on the shore by the hundreds to watch the unfolding drama. It was war as spectator sport. "No moving picture manager could have staged a sea battle more effectually for the summer visitors," reported the *New York Times*. Even as the attack continued, boats dispatched from shore started picking up survivors. Other passengers and crew from the barges, including women and children, had taken to lifeboats and were rowing hard for shore.

Riding so low in the water, the barges did not make easy targets. Some of the shells from the deck gun overshot the mark and landed on shore and in the marsh behind the town, but others hit home and exploded a shower of splintered wood. The spectators did not stir. They were amazed that such an attack was taking place in the sleepy waters of Nauset Bay, but equally amazed that it could happen at all and that nothing was being done about it.

Where was the greatest navy on earth, promised by the government? There was a naval station at nearby Provincetown. They had been on heightened alert since the U-boat attacks began in U.S. waters. Did they have ships on the way? In anticipation of a threat to its coastline, the United States had invested heavily in coastal defenses. Airplanes and dirigibles maintained constant patrol, flying out of a network of air stations like the one at Chatham. An improved wireless and telephone network allowed for faster response to any threat. These stations had been designed to prevent exactly the sort of attack happening at Nauset Bay. Word had in fact reached the Provincetown Naval Station, which dispatched a flotilla of fifty-one speedy submarine chasers.

To the delight of the spectators, the large seaplanes from the Chatham Naval Air Station swooped in over the hori-

10. Created specifically to deal with U-boats in coastal waters, the sub chaser was built of wood and armed with two three-inch guns and two machine guns. Later versions carried a depth charge launcher or Y-gun as well as an underwater hydrophone for detecting engine and propeller noise.
Library of Congress

zon. Intent on their work, the crew of U-156 did not see the planes until they had the sub squarely in their sights. As the first plane nosed down for attack, the U-156 crew scrambled to get off the deck and submerge. Ensign Shields, pilot of one of the seaplanes, would later report on the encounter.

> I had the sight dead on the deck and pulled the release [for the bomb]; it failed to work. I waved a signal to fly back at a lower altitude, and as the plane came down upon the submarine again . . . Howard [aboard the plane] tested the release: it stuck. A moment more and we would be yards out of range. Howard sprang out of the cockpit into the blast of wind . . . [and] leaning head downward he released

the bomb, under the wing with his fingers. It was all done so quickly the pilots did not know what he was about. The bomb, with its charge of TNT dropped straight and splashed within a few feet of the U-boat. It did not explode.

U-156 resurfaced and fired shrapnel shells at the aircraft. A second plane, piloted by Captain Eaton, began a zigzag dive, dodging shrapnel bursts. Pilots were advised not to drop their bombs at less than one thousand feet for fear the concussion would rip the fabric off the wings. But Eaton dove to four hundred feet before releasing his bomb, which fell within yards of the U-boat, close enough to crush its hull, but that bomb also failed to explode. One of the aviators would later claim that he had been so frustrated by his inability to stop the attack that he grabbed the monkey wrench from his on board toolbox and dropped it on the submarine.

When those who witnessed the attack later told their stories, hundreds of onlookers registered different sights and impressions than the tugboat captain, the crew members on the barges, the Coast Guard men watching from their tower, and the aviators charged with destroying the submarine. The observers disputed how many planes appeared, how many bombs were dropped, whether the planes drove the submarine away or the U-boat merely departed after finishing its work. The varying stories, clouded by anger, frustration, and fear, were symptomatic of the U.S. Navy's encounters with the U-boats in general, as though both the degree of threat and the effectiveness of the navy's response were open to interpretation.

To drive home that point, the citizens of Orleans took the visit of U-156 in stride. The day after the attack a makeshift sign appeared on the bluffs commemorating the event, and neighborhood children turned the site into a tourist attraction, charging visitors ten cents to look over the bluff at the location where the attack occurred. One homeowner maintained a sign on his property well into the 1930s that read "Only German shells of W.W. I to land on U.S. soil landed on the marsh below, fired by U-56 [U-156] on July 21, 1918." The event lives in town legend to this day.

Regardless of the seriousness of the attack, the indisputable facts were that U-156 had remained on the scene for ninety minutes, fired 147 rounds, finished its business unscathed, and then leisurely sailed back to the open ocean. And what was truly inconceivable to many was that it did all of this within miles of a Coast Guard station, a naval base, and a naval air station.

The sub chasers sent out to save the day never appeared. The commander of the flotilla, overcome by an abundance of caution at the thought of confronting U-156's big deck guns, turned around and returned to base before even seeing the U-boat. The navy would not have another such golden opportunity to strike a blow at the U-boats assaulting the United States.

U-156 finished its American mission by attacking fishing boats from Cape Cod to the Bay of Fundy, sinking twenty-one of them. None of these sinkings resulted from the stereotypic ambush torpedo attack. The means of attack was either to board the vessel and plant explosives or send it to the bottom with shellfire from the deck gun after giving the crew time to board lifeboats.

As with the earlier U-151, survivors brought to shore stories of the attacks, which had become a newspaper staple. Each story added a new twist to the U-boat saga, glimpses of German humanity or cruelty, idiosyncrasies of the encounter, harrowing days adrift at sea. Typically the U-boat boarding parties spoke English. In fact, a German officer told one group of survivors that he had owned a summer home in Maine since 1896 and that he had lived in America a long time. Another of the German officers claimed that he had captained a tug boat in that area before the war.

The fact that some of the U-boat crew had lived in New England seemed to explain how U-156 could navigate tricky coastal waters so well. Such facts also fed the paranoia about German Americans, many of whom had sympathized with the German cause early in the war. The expulsion in 1915 of the German military attaché Franz von Papen and the Austrian ambassador Constantin Dumba uncovered networks of German agents intent on disrupting the manufacture of war matériel. The year 1916 gave proof to the effectiveness of German espionage when a catastrophic explosion destroyed the Black Tom munitions facility in Jersey City.

In the wake of the visits by U-151 and U-156, German Americans came under suspicion of aiding the attacks. Some had already been arrested in the Nauset Bay area and in Atlantic City for possessing coastal maps or for suspicion of signaling the U-boats with lights or laundry hanging on a line.

U-156 headed home from its successful mission in late August having sunk thirty-four ships weighing a total of 33,582 tons. Because of the number of ships sunk, the very public Nauset Bay attack, and the sinking of a warship with a mine, U-156 made a huge impression on the public. The audacity of its attacks seemed a frightening escalation of the U-boat war on America. Congress introduced a resolution on August 12 requesting answers from the secretary of the navy. How could it be that for nearly two months, U-156 seemed able to do whatever it wanted, wherever it wanted, and the U.S. Navy was powerless to stop it? If a U-boat could operate in American waters with such impunity, no one knew what to expect next.

As the weeks dragged on and the pattern of the U-boat attacks became clearer, public hysteria eased. No critical convoys were attacked, the U-boats instead contenting themselves with commerce raiding. As distressing and frustrating as that was, the toll of fishing boats, unarmed schooners, passenger liners, and a small number of transports was microscopic compared to the tonnage destroyed by U-boats in European waters, and incidental to America's commitment to supply the war. In fact, the U-boat attacks had not distracted from the key strategic objective of maintaining the continuous shipment of men and matériel to the war front.

In August, while U-156 finished its mission of shelling barges and sinking fishing vessels, 140 troop ships carried 286,375 men to France. The success of the transport effort was already helping to turn the tide of the war. The first large-scale involvement of American troops occurred that summer. In July, the Allied counterattack in the Second Battle of the Marne included eight divisions of U.S. troops. The Battle of Amien, on August 8, became known as the Black Day for the German Army, since reverses on the battlefield extinguished any hope of a German victory.

Would German setbacks in the land war now motivate U-boats to confront American convoys?

The Summer U-Boat Assault Continues

America was now held hostage by German "super-submarines," a *New York Times* article reported on August 16. Under construction as merchant submarines, U-151 and U-156 had been converted to combat vessels with the addition of external torpedo tubes, armored hulls, and six-inch deck guns. They far outmatched any armed merchant ship, in fact these super-subs could hold their own in surface combat with any warship up to a battle cruiser.

An oil tanker fell victim to a U-boat the day before that warning article appeared, as had a coal ship six miles off the coast. One captain reported that when the first shells splashed down before his vessel, signaling him to stop, he had no idea where they came from, as no ship was in sight. But he knew the drill only too well and hurried his crew into

11. The U-155 that operated off the U.S. coast in 1918 was the former merchant U-boat *Deutschland*, converted to a combat vessel. It represented a class of giant U-cruisers that Germany created in the last year of the war. It is pictured here on display in London after the war. U.S. Signal Corps

the lifeboats and rowed hard to put distance between him and his vessel. By the time seaplanes and submarine chasers arrived on the scene, the ship was sunk and the U-boat gone.

The book *The U-boat Hunters* appeared in June 1918, at the frenzied opening of the U-boat attacks on the United States, to capitalize on the public's intense interest in the submarine war. Author James B. Connolly warned that Germany's cruiser U-boats increased the likelihood of an invasion of America. The threat of a land invasion of the United States did not resonate with the public as it might have a few years earlier. Educated by four years of obsessive war news and newspaper accounts of U-boat warfare, the public had left behind the high anxiety of the invasion novels and movies of 1915 and 1916.

In the popular 1915 novel *America Fallen!: The Sequel to the European War,* by J. Bernard Walker, German submarines simultaneously attack the navy in New York, the Panama Canal Zone, Boston, Norfolk, Charleston, and Pensacola, destroying all U.S. warships and submarines as a prelude to a German invasion. Such an invasion was unlikely to take place as long as the British navy kept the German fleet barricaded in port. However, the full evil intent of the U-boats then in American waters was not yet clear. Attacking freighters and passenger ships was troubling enough, but attacking ships in a harbor and shelling the shore bore an echo of *America Fallen!*

Since the navy alone stood between the attackers and the home front, the public tallied an informal scorecard of success, matching the frequent accounts of sinking ships against reports of navy maneuvers, strategies, and the new technology being thrown into the fight. The navy continued to ramp up its defensive measures and instituted new tactics. Airplanes, dirigibles, kite balloons (small tethered blimps), and ships maintained constant patrols and surveillance. Merchant ships received instructions on how to avoid or escape from a U-boat, such as zigzagging or running without lights at night. Armed merchants ships proved an effective deterrent. Other measures included smoke screens that allowed ships or convoys to conceal their movements. Camouflaging ships gave them a low-visibility profile. Since ships belching smoke from their funnels attracted attention on the horizon, the use of smokeless coal made them harder to sight.

The United States borrowed from the British the use of Q-ships, freighters that carried hidden guns and employed a strategy that invited their own destruction to draw their attacker close. Merchant ship decoys were also used in conjunction with American submarines that would lurk underwater and then turn the tables on an attacking U-boat.

The four-masted schooner *George Whittimore* served as a Q-ship, sailing with an American submarine up and down the New Jersey coast for over a month without success. All of these measures would be tested over the summer of 1918.

Making the Run to the War Zone

Throughout the summer, an endless procession of ships made the run to British and French ports and back—typically taking two weeks to make the crossing—under constant threat of attack. They sailed from New York, Norfolk, and Boston to rendezvous points off the coast, where they gathered into convoys. Planes, blimps, and warships escorted them to a collection point, where they came under the protection of a cruiser and an armed merchant assigned to take them across.

A ship's lookout served as its first line of defense. By this point in the war, the transport service had watchfulness down to a science. No transport ship had enough crew for the task, so others on board were recruited. As suggested in *The U-boat Hunters*, it was not unusual for some midwestern farm boy turned soldier who had never stepped foot on a ship—or ever seen the ocean—to find himself being tutored by a ship's officer in the fine points of spotting U-boats, and then soon standing at the railing or one hundred feet up in the crow's nest peering intently through binoculars for some telltale speck on the ocean.

Ship's lookouts maintained a twenty-four-hour vigil with numerous men who each had responsibility for only a fifteen degree sector. Working in thirty minute shifts to maintain concentration, they continually monitored their narrow portion of the sea. U-boats came within a thousand yards of their prey for an attack. If the ship was being stalked by a U-boat, the lookout hoped to glimpse the black stick of the periscope lifted perhaps a foot above the surface of the water, or the white line that the periscope cut through the water as the U-boat commander took a quick observation. A good U-boat skipper needed to run up his periscope for only five or six seconds to have a look and judge the attack. The periscope might project for twenty to thirty seconds during the actual attack.

If a lookout spotted a periscope the convoy would abruptly change course, and the escort vessels would rush to depth charge the spot. If the periscope went unseen, the torpedo might be on its way. A torpedo cut a white wake across the surface. If given sufficient alert, the captain could turn the vessel hard to run parallel to the course of the torpedo, making the ship a smaller target.

When the convoy arrived within a few hundred miles of the French or British coast, waters heavy with U-boats, more lookouts were added. Attacks came often in these waters. Ships ran dark at night and sailed a zigzag course, and their captains spent every waking hour on the bridge. "I should not say that there was much fear aboard," claimed Irvin S. Cobb, reporter for the *Saturday Evening Post*, making the crossing in February 1918, "but there was a sort of nagging, persistent sense of uneasiness betraying itself in various small ways. For one thing, all of us made more jokes about submarines, mines and other perils of the deep than was natural. There was something a little forced, artificial, about this gaiety—laughs came from the lips, but not from points further south."

Many of the soldiers on troop ships slept in their clothing and kept their life vests close at hand so they could respond quickly to an attack. In these coastal waters, the escort ships handed over their duties to a flotilla of destroyers or sub chasers that came out to meet the convoy and escort it to harbor. Irvin Cobb reported the relief felt by his fellow passengers when they came within sight of the Irish coast. But it was precisely in this more protected zone that the ship immediately behind his in the convoy got torpedoed. Cobb huddled on deck with fellow passengers to watch the struggles of the U.S. troopship *Tuscania*, suddenly brilliantly alight, as the distance between the two ships increased. "We could feel our ship throb under our feet as she picked up speed. It made us feel like cowards. Near at hand a ship was in distress, a ship laden with a precious freightage of American soldier boys, and here were we legging it like a frightened bird, weaving in and out on sharp tacks."

Several red rocket flares illuminated the sky, appeals for help from the stricken *Tuscania*, just before Cobb noticed the ship's lights make a noticeable tilt as it went down by the bow. "There was silence among us as we watched. None of us, I take it, had words within him to express what he felt; so we said nothing at all, but just stared out across the waters until our eyeballs ached in their sockets."

Rescue did come for most of the *Tuscania* passengers, though over 250 lost their lives. Because American troopships were so well protected in convoys, U-boats sank only three of them during the war. The loss of any ship in a convoy drove home the vulnerability of the transport effort.

Heading Home

The American oil tanker *O.B. Jennings* survived the U-boat gauntlet off the English coast to deliver its cargo and was homebound to Newport News, Virginia. Ships loaded with men and war matériel heading to the war zone received escort, but those returning empty usually travelled on their own; all the more reason they had to remain especially vigilant and employ every strategy to avoid or survive a U-boat attack.

Running some sixty miles off the U.S. coast on August 4, 1918, *Jennings*'s captain George Nordstrom spotted the rippling wake of a torpedo running straight toward his vessel. He made a hard swing of the helm, held his breath, and watched the torpedo pass by harmlessly. At 10,289 tons, the *Jennings* was a large ship for the day and carried a four-inch gun manned by a British gun crew. The ship sent out a distress call and put on full speed on a zigzag course to make itself a more difficult target. The attacking U-boat surfaced and opened fire with its six-inch gun. The *Jennings* deployed smoke boxes to screen itself from its attacker and fired its own gun, employing everything available in an armed freighter's arsenal of escape. All to no avail. After taking several direct hits from the attacking U-boat, the *Jennings* struck its colors, and the crew took to the lifeboats.

The *Jennings* had just encountered another of the U-boats operating off the coast. Even before U-156 departed, two more German submarines, U-140 and U-117 arrived off the coast, plus a third U-boat very familiar to U.S. waters was on the way, U-155, the former *Deutschland*. The merchant submarine that had twice visited the United States for trading purposes in 1916 had been converted to a combat vessel with the addition of torpedo tubes and deck guns.

The U-boat that shelled the *Jennings*, U-140, represented the epitome of U-boat development, making it more than a match for the luckless armed tanker. At 302 feet in length and with a 29 foot beam, U-140 was the largest submarine afloat. Unlike the converted merchant submarines, U-140 had been designed from scratch as a combat vessel. A cruising range of thirty-two thousand miles gave it the capability of long missions, and an impressive surface speed of twenty-six knots meant that it could catch up with any ship attempting an escape. With two six-inch deck guns it could stand up against anything short of a major warship. Its mission in U.S. waters was to destroy large transports.

Germans considered any armed merchant boat to be a warship. So, when U-140 came up to the *Jennings*'s lifeboats to determine the ship's identity, it took as a prisoner of war one of the *Jennings*'s officers, Rene Bastin. Bastin would travel aboard the U-boat for the rest of its mission and then be taken back to Germany and held as prisoner. After the armistice ended hostilities, Bastin returned to the United States and published an account of his adventures. Among his revelations, he claimed to have witnessed the destruction of U-156, the submarine that shelled the tug boat and barges in Nauset Bay. Sailing with U-140 on the return voyage, U-156 struck an American mine at the northern entrance to the North Sea. American readers found ironic satisfaction in the fact that the U-boat that had planted the mine that sank the cruiser *San Diego* had itself been destroyed by a mine.

The U.S. destroyer *Hull* picked up the *Jennings*'s distress call and raced to the scene, but by the time it arrived the *Jennings* already rested on the ocean floor, and U-140 had moved on to its next victim. Even though the navy had heightened its efforts and expanded the resources committed to the hunt, this same cat-and-mouse scenario repeated itself with frustrating regularity.

When wireless operators at naval radio stations along the Virginia and North Carolina coasts captured the desperate SOS calls from ships under attack, or the reported sightings of U-boats, lifeboats, or debris, the navy scrambled a seaplane, a submarine chaser, or a destroyer. Typically, they arrived on the scene in time to rescue survivors. Occasionally, their appearance forced a U-boat to break off an attack and flee the scene. Despite the best efforts of ships' captains and coastal defenders, the U-140 went about its deadly business little troubled.

Down went the *Stanley S. Seaman* and the *Diamond Shoals Light* vessel on August 6. The ships' wireless SOS transmissions sent nearby freighters steaming full speed from the area. The U-boat chased and shelled them, sinking the American steamer *Merak*. U-140 was having a field day.

Survivors of the *Diamond Shoals* attack claimed that the U-boat had fired poison gas shells. That was not true, but it fed the prevailing image of German barbarity. Residents in some coastal communities, already made nervous by the sound of repeated gunfire off the coast, asked the government for gas masks.

"Other sinkings will probably follow," was the fatalistic response from Secretary Daniels. Interviewed during U-140's activities, he explained that the mission of the U-boats was to hinder commerce as much as possible without exposing themselves to danger.

Debate about German U-boat strategy and the American response simmered over the summer. Calls to bring back destroyers from the war zone to better protect against the marauding U-boats met with resistance from the navy. The United States had already begun to consider these U-boat activities as devilish annoyances that must be endured in the pursuit of the war. German strategy clearly meant to distract the United States from full pursuit of the war in Europe. If the U-boat attacks on America could draw off warships from the North Sea, they would have done their job. Daniels's rationale made perfect strategic sense, but offered little comfort to a nervous public as the attacks continued.

U-140 got an early start the following morning. "SOS 36° N. 73° W. Help." Coastal radio stations picked up the distress call from the Brazilian passenger liner *Uberaba*. "We are running extreme danger. We are being attacked." Shells from the U-boat's six-inch guns exploded geysers near the ship as it fled on a zigzag course. Passengers gathered on deck in preparation to abandon ship, but shrapnel shells forced them below again. A radio message that destroyers were rushing to the scene encouraged the *Uberaba* to hold out against the attack. A passenger ship under attack was an especially distressing situation as it imperiled hundreds of people, mainly civilians likely to include women and children. The destroyer USS *Stringham* appeared on the scene so quickly that it was able to drop depth charges on the spot where the U-boat had just submerged.

U-140 went on a high-angle crash dive to 100 feet. According to Rene Bastin, then a prisoner on board, the jarring detonations of depth charges forced the sub to 300 feet. There the concussion of a nearby explosion sent a shock wave through the submarine, forcing it still lower, below 400 feet. The large U-boat had been tested for 495 feet, but damage from the explosions had loosened U-140's rivets and opened joints. Fountains of water sprayed the interior, and the ship tilted first one way then the other.

The crew scrambled to gain control of leaks and rig emergency power. Miraculously, it held on until the following day when it surfaced to a clear sea and could assess the extensive damage. The deck and conning tour had buckled, and one of the six-inch guns had torn from its mounting, as had the wireless antenna. Serious oil leaks already blotched the sea with telltale slicks that would allow airplanes or ships to follow its every move. The captain had no choice but to plot a slow return to Germany. The U.S. Navy was not aware of it, but it had finally scored a victory against a U-boat.

Victories against U-boats were indeed few. The most stunning score for the United States had come the previous November when the destroyers USS *Fanning* and USS *Nicholson* engaged U-58 in the North Atlantic, damaging it with depth charges and shellfire and forcing it to surrender. Its crew now languished in a Georgia POW camp. The navy, however, would record no such triumphs in East Coast waters.

Civilian Ideas to Combat U-Boats

At the start of the Great War, the British admiralty had imagined that naval warfare would involve a clash of fleets. Nations defined their naval prowess by the number and size of their dreadnaught battleships. But in this war, clashes of surface vessels had been rare, and surface naval battles even rarer. Instead the conflict between surface ships and submarines defined the naval war following a seesaw of technical advances, new strategies, and inventions that slowly tipped the hand in favor of the defender.

The technological improvement of German submarines gave them the capability of traveling further and faster, going deeper and staying submerged longer, with larger guns and more mines and torpedoes. The Allies responded rapidly with new weapons aimed specifically at the submarine threat. Blimps and kite balloons offered a lofty perch for sighting distant U-boats on the surface. Speedy new vessels, such as the submarine chaser and destroyer, were developed precisely for submarine warfare. They could respond quickly to any attack or reported sighting and then drop another new weapon, the depth charge, underwater bombs containing three hundred to six hundred pounds of TNT that could be set to explode at various depths. Their crushing concussions were capable of breaching the hulls of submarines. The invention of the Y-gun allowed ships to throw off depth charges in pairs to either side of the attacking surface vessel. The hydrophone, an underwater listening device, could detect a submerged submarine.

By this point in the war, the general public had acquired a thorough education in submarine warfare, an education based on sensationalism, propaganda, technology, and the relentless parade of reported attacks. They knew of the Herculean efforts to counter U-boats in European waters. Special interest magazines and professional journals provided considerable technical details about submarines and the weapons to fight them. The challenge of countering U-boats stirred the imaginations of thousands of scientists, inventors, tinkerers, crackpots, and ordinary citizens. When the British set up a civilian Board of Invention and Research to

12. An observer climbs a rope into the basket suspended below
an observation kite balloon at the U.S. Naval Air Station,
Hampton Roads, Virginia. Kite balloons were used to watch
for U-boat activity off the coast. Library of Congress

evaluate ideas from the public as to how to counter submarines, fourteen thousand suggestions poured in.

Even before America entered the war, it enlisted a group
of scientists, engineers, and inventors into a Naval Consulting Board to harness their collective genius to solve some of
the problems facing the navy, chief among them being the
U-boat threat. To head this august body, Secretary Daniels
selected America's most high-profile genius—Thomas Edison. Although seventy years old, Edison became captivated
by the challenge. He spent several months on a naval vessel on Long Island Sound experimenting with techniques
for detecting submarines. Congress appropriated funds
for the creation of a naval research laboratory where new
ideas could be developed and tested. During the course of
the war, the public flooded the board with more than one
hundred thousand suggestions.

It became a well-established notion with the public that new inventions and weapons lay on the horizon that would neutralize the U-boat. In 1916 the magazine *The Electrical Experimenter* reported that the inventor Nikola Tesla could destroy naval vessels with electrical waves. Using the large Tesla wireless tower located at Shoreham, Long Island, radio waves of sufficient intensity could be directed at enemy ships in our waters that would blow them to atoms. No such device ever appeared.

Shortly after U.S. entry into the war, newspapers reported that Elmer Sperry, creator of the gyroscope, had invented a device to counter submarines. Not so, claimed the secretary of the Naval Consulting Board, Thomas Robbins. The board reviewed many inventions, and developed some to be tested, but none yet existed to counter the U-boat. "If the inventors of this country are able to devise something which will beat the submarine," he patiently explained, "the first people to be informed of the fact should be the crew of a German submarine."

One of the most promising lines of research undertaken by the board involved the detection of submarines by means of "supersonics," a precursor of sonar. In October 1918, U.S. experts met with their Allied counterparts in Paris to discuss this promising research. However, the navy would not benefit from this important technology or any other research from the board. The end game was playing out too rapidly to await further inventions.

Throughout September and October, the final two U-boats destined to attack America, U-155 and U-152, operated along the U.S. coast. The deadliest encounter between a U-boat and an American ship unfolded when U-152 came upon the USS *Ticonderoga* straggling behind a Europe-bound convoy. The freighter carried a cargo of railroad ties, 115 soldiers, and a crew of 124.

The *Ticonderoga* came out on the losing end of a two-

13. The Naval Consulting Board, consisting of scientists, engineers, and inventors, advised the navy on how to deal with U-boats. Thomas Edison, front center, headed the board. To his left stands Navy Secretary Daniels. Far right in the front row is the assistant secretary of the navy, Franklin Roosevelt. Library of Congress

hour gun battle. Even after the ship hoisted a white flag of surrender, shrapnel rounds from the U-boat killed and wounded many of the men and destroyed most of the lifeboats. The U-boat took two officers prisoner. A life raft and its ten men fell victim to a storm. On the fourth day, a ship rescued twenty-four survivors from the only other lifeboat and returned them to America, where they added their horrific story to the chronicles of the U-boat war.

Other encounters with the two U-boats played out moment by moment on the airways in heart-pounding drama. When the British steamer *Reginolite* came under fire from U-155 on October 6, it tried to escape and sent out regular radio alerts during the attack—Being gunned by submarine, returning fire, zigzagging, shells landing close. Shore stations and ships in the area followed the encounter with bated breath, through fifteen minutes of radio silence, until the ship finally reported that it had opened distance from the submarine and was escaping.

While U-152 and U-155 frustrated the navy with continuing attacks, the cruiser submarine U-139 began its mission to America. The mammoth craft, nearly four hundred feet long, was commanded by Germany's number one U-boat ace, Arnauld de la Perière. His record of two hundred ships sunk far surpassed any other submarine commander. As skipper of U-35 in the Mediterranean, he sank several British and French troop transports, resulting in the death of thousands of soldiers. U-139 took the name of *Commander Schweiger*, in honor of the U-boat commander who sank the *Lusitania*.

On October 1, on his way to America, Perière sank three ships in a convoy off the coast of Spain, but a depth charge attack from the escorting cruisers disabled the U-boat's periscopes. That loss would prevent the U-boat from conducting any submerged attacks. Undaunted, U-139 sank a ship near the Azores with gunfire then continued west.

But Perière never made it to America. On October 20, when U-139 stood halfway across the Atlantic, the German naval base at Kiel broadcast a wireless order for all U-boats to return home. Things were unraveling quickly for Germany. Its army was being rolled back under the assault of the combined Allied armies that included an infusion of hundreds of thousands of fresh American troops.

On October 28, mutiny erupted throughout the German High Seas Fleet, and defiant sailors quickly took over the naval base at Kiel. The armistice brought an end to hostilities on November 11. By the time Arnauld de la Perière sailed U-139 into Kiel on November 14, rebellious sailors and soldiers had spread a Russian-style revolution throughout much of the military and many cities. U-155 and U-152 arrived from America the next day. Other U-boats continued to straggle back to their bases or surrendered in neutral or allied ports. Under the terms of the armistice, every U-boat—the entire German fleet—had to be surrendered to the Allies. Within one week the German submarine fleet that had so terrorized the seas and nearly won the war would venture to an appointed location in the North Sea, surrender to British crews, and sail peacefully into the English port of Harwich.

4

DELIVERED INTO ALLIED HANDS

The 20th of November 1918 will ever rank as an anniversary
without precedent in the history of sea warfare. For upon
that date the first installment of the German submarines
surrendered to the British Navy in general, and to the
British Submarine Service in particular.
—Stephen King-Hall, *A North Sea Diary, 1914–1918*

The British destroyers *Melampus* and *Firedrake* put out from
Harwich, England predawn on November 20, 1918, making
their way cautiously through heavy fog. On board they carried the largest single collection of submarine officers and
crew ever assembled in one location and an equally impressive collection of reporters, photographers, and cinematographers. They had gathered from all over England over
the previous few days, giddy with the end of the war and
the historic event in which they were about to play a part.

The two destroyers steamed past the boom and net at
the harbor entrance. Such booms guarded every harbor in
Britain as protection from the dreaded U-boats. As dawn
broke and the fog thinned, a British airship sailed majes-
tically overhead then droned off to the north.

Article XXII of the armistice, signed on November 11,
called for the surrender of all German naval vessels. The next
day Germany's High Seas Fleet would turn itself over to an
enormous assemblage of Allied warships and be escorted
into internment at the large British naval base at Scapa Flow.
But this day belonged to the submarines, and their surrender would serve as a rehearsal for how well Germany's

proud navy would submit to this humiliation. There had been no culminating engagement to decide the naval war. And now the undefeated, remarkably successful U-boats were expected to give themselves up to their enemy.

A British force of five cruisers and twenty destroyers had left the night before to wait at the point of surrender, ready for any Hun treachery. *Melampus* and *Firedrake* arrived just before the appointed hour of 10:00 a.m. to join in the vigil. The line of destroyers stretched for several miles, and on all of them sailors crowded the decks, peering hard into the mist. In a way the ritual was a curious reenactment of exactly what these men had devoted themselves to during the war—stalking the dangerous and elusive U-boats.

Aboard the *Firedrake* a startled lookout yelled, "By Jove, there's a ruddy Fritz!" causing a rush to the port side that caused the ship to list. It took a keen eye to discern that first dark silhouette emerging from the mist, its dome-shaped conning tower perched upon a thin line in the water. Several more soon appeared in a straggling line. With their crews lining their decks, they made their way toward the British ships, where they came to a stop. There were twenty in this installment. Many more would follow in the coming days.

News cameras flashed and movie cameras rolled, capturing the infamous U-boats, at last defanged. The British sailors witnessing this spectacle were dumbstruck. Parked before them was the adversary that had nearly brought the British Empire to its knees. Many of the sailors had been bitterly fighting U-boats for four years but never seen one. Now the infamous vessels had sailed up peacefully and parked beneath the British guns.

A British submarine officer was the first to board each U-boat and curtly run through the brief formalities for transfer of the vessel. The admiralty had already drawn up a list of U-boat commanders that it planned to hold accountable for their crimes, including the infamous Wilhelm Werner, "who excels in sinking of hospital ships." But none of the wanted commanders were found.

British crews went aboard the submarines to take them into harbor. Orders had been issued forbidding any demonstration, and these were followed to the letter. With the German crews remaining on deck, the submarines sailed into Harwich displaying the white ensign of surrender above the German flag. Spectators crowded the ships in the harbor, but they maintained a complete silence as though they watched the funeral cortege of some great person rather than the defeat of an enemy they had fought so bitterly for four years. The German sailors were transferred to a German destroyer and transported home.

The reporter for the *New York Sun*, witnessing these events, summed up the finality in these terms, "The last event of the day was seeing the German submarines, now purged of crews, lying in bunches of three securely moored in the inner harbor of Harwich. It was growing dark, and their curious ghastly shapes recalled other ghosts—ghosts of women and children and merchant seaman—pallid, bloodless human faces floating onto the lift of the water in the gray deserted wastes of the Atlantic."

The next day, nineteen more U-boats surrendered, and twenty-one on the day after that. Over the next few weeks they trickled in until 176 of them moored in row after row at what came to be called "U-boat Avenue."

The U.S. Navy Gets Its U-Boats

British naval officer Stephen King-Hall, who participated in the surrender, wrote that the most outstanding feature of all the U-boats was their filthy condition. "How much of this is normal and how much is due to present conditions in the German Fleet, it is difficult to say. I personally find it quite hard to go round some of the boats without being almost physically sick." Many of the boats had not been

14. A British officer inspects the papers of a surrendered German U-boat. British crews went on board to sail the vessels into the naval base at Harwich, England. *The War of the Nations: Portfolio in Rotogravure*, Library of Congress

properly maintained in the final months of the war. The German crews had also engaged in vandalism and sabotage of critical equipment.

Maintaining the U-boats became an immediate challenge for the British. Since plans were to eventually distribute the boats among the Allies, they had to be kept in working order. Batteries had to be kept charged, water leaks plugged, and the boats had to be guarded against a persistent army of souvenir hunters and vandals. These latter prowled U-boat Avenue, sneaking onto the boats and stripping them of periscope optics, compasses, and other high value items.

Some of the submarines also opened to a curious public so they could see the fearful weapons that had haunted their imagination throughout the war. Crowds came aboard and pulled levers and threw switches and turned wheels and valves, inadvertently damaging machinery and even sinking some boats.

Allied representatives quickly set off for Germany to assure that all naval vessels had been surrendered or accounted for. There they found some U-boats inoperable or still under construction in German yards. Germany had been on an accelerated building campaign in the closing months of the war, still pushing innovation and new technology in the desperate hope that their U-boats could turn the tide of the war, or at least make the terms of surrender more advantageous.

Although a few U-boats had also surrendered at various Allied ports, the 176 submarines at Harwich represented virtually the entire fleet of operable German submarines. While discussion swirled about how shipping companies would be compensated for their huge losses from the U-boats and which U-boat captains would be prosecuted for war crimes, Allied naval officials and engineers swooped in for a close look at the treasure that had been delivered into their hands. U.S. naval officers who saw the German submarines were uniformly impressed. Powerful and sturdy diesel engines, superior periscope optics, and the double hull construction that better protected them from depth charges set the German boats above those in the Allied navies.

The surrendered boats contained samples of the three main types of U-boats developed during the war: the small UB coastal attack boats, UC minelayers, and the large ocean-going U-cruisers. They offered the Allies a golden opportunity to learn German technology so that it could be incorporated into the next generation of their own submarines.

In December the United States formed a Submarine Inspection Board to conduct a detailed examination of select U-boats. They reviewed each class of boat, including the U-53, famous for visiting Newport prior to U.S.

entry into the war, and the giant U-cruiser U-140 that had recently raided the U.S. coast, which they examined in dry dock at Kiel, Germany.

The board took four boats to the waters off Dorset for three weeks of intensive technical evaluation. Their findings only confirmed the impressions of others who had inspected the German boats. Although they offered terrible living conditions for the crew, they were remarkably reliable and technically superior to U.S. submarines. It seemed imperative at that point that the United States take possession of some of the U-boats to more fully examine their construction.

In February, U.S. commander Emory Land wrote to Secretary Daniels, strongly urging that the United States acquire some of these vessels for closer inspection at home. The other Allied countries had reached the same conclusion. In fact they were already sailing away with their prizes. Japan had sent home two U-boats on February 18 and was preparing six more for departure in early March. France was slated to get forty-six of the vessels and Italy ten. To the great frustration of Land and other submarine officers, the Navy Department showed little interest in acquiring any of the U-boats.

Back in the United States the director of submarines, Cpt. Thomas Hart, urged the same action on the chief of naval operations, William S. Benson, but met the same lack of interest. For a number of reasons, studying the technical merits of German submarines was not a high priority. For one, Benson believed that new technologies to combat the submarine would eventually make it obsolete. But before that even happened, the nations of the world might outlaw the submarine along with poison gas. Moreover, the moral issue might make the move unpopular. Why did America want to improve upon and adopt the very weapon that sank the *Lusitania*, hospital and passenger ships, and unarmed merchant ships? Britain already had plans to prosecute some U-boat commanders for engaging in unlawful warfare.

For Hart, already convinced of the superiority of the German submarines, acquiring some U-boats was simply too great an opportunity to pass up. To his way of thinking, the inhumane use of submarines was more a reflection of German character than of the weapon itself. Furthermore, how did one differentiate between submarines and other even more devastating engines of war, such as the bomb, mine, gas, or torpedo? He estimated that submarines were responsible for some 12,800 deaths over the course of a war that saw eight million fatalities. As he saw it, "many single days of the land warfare cost us a bigger loss of life than that and with far less decisive results." A smart naval officer had to acknowledge that a few hundred German submarines had come perilously close to winning the war.

Operating outside official channels, Hart took advantage of some highly-placed civilian contacts in Washington DC to tie the U-boats to the pending war bond drive. The United States had partly financed its involvement in the war through the sale of war bonds. Four Liberty Loan drives during the war brought in $4 billion. The drives proved successful because they became symbols of every citizen's patriotic duty and because they were creatively and aggressively marketed. Hollywood stars, Boy Scouts and Girl Scouts, barnstorming army aviators, and a pervasive network of hometown bond committees whipping up community pride to meet their sales quotas all proved effective marketing tools.

Now that the war was over, the final expenses would be paid off with one final bond drive, this time renamed the Victory Loan. To recapture the strong strain of patriotism that motivated sales on the earlier drives, campaign organizers brought back war trophies from Europe to aid the cause. "War exhibit trains" of captured enemy weapons visited cities and small towns to be featured at bond rallies. In some communities, those buying a $1,000 bond would receive a captured German helmet. Tens of thousands of the infamous spiked helmets were distributed and still populate antique shops and auctions to this day. As an incentive to individual communities, the campaign promised one of the captured German war trophies to every community that oversubscribed its bond quota with at least 20 percent of its population subscribing. A town could receive a machine gun or an artillery piece to dress up the local cemetery or park.

"What is the best war trophy available?" Captain Hart asked Victory Loan officials. The answer of course was the very symbol of the naval war, the weapon that drew the United States into the war: the hated, the dreaded German U-boat.

A U-boat had been used to promote bond sales once before with great success. The British sent the captured mine-laying U-boat UC-5 to the United States in 1917. At New York, bond drive officials cut the submarine into three pieces and hauled them by horse-drawn wagon to Central Park, where the boat was reassembled and renamed "U-Buy-a-Bond." For the first time, Americans saw an actual U-boat up close and—for the price of a war bond—they could explore its interior. The event drew huge crowds and spurred bond sales.

Captain Hart suggested bringing several of the recently-surrendered U-boats to the United States and sending them around to every coastal city to sell bonds from their decks. The novel idea appealed to Victory Loan officials, who worried about selling bonds at a time when wartime patriotism was waning. Hart's idea quickly won their endorsement. In less than twelve hours, orders came down from the secretary of the navy to bring the U-boats to America.

Everything kicked into high gear in March 1919. Using the Victory Loan campaign as an excuse to acquire the

U-boats imposed a tight schedule on the crews that would man them. The Victory Loan campaign would officially commence on April 21 and run through May 10. Twelve naval officers and 120 enlisted men hurried off to England in March. Most of the sea traffic headed in the opposite direction during this time, as thousands of troops streamed home from Europe.

The navy team boarded an ex-German passenger liner, the *Kronprinzessin Cecille*, and had the ship to themselves. Officer Charles Lockwood would later recall in his book *Down to the Sea in Subs* the luxurious accommodations they enjoyed, the sweeping staircases, the sumptuous dining saloon, and the many gold-framed pictures of bosomy blondes.

Accommodations were not so grand for them in Harwich. The submarine tender USS *Bushnell* waited there to provide quarters. However, because it was not large enough to house all of the men, a few of the lucky officers passed over to the luxurious yacht, *Harvard*, which had served as an antisubmarine escort vessel in the Channel and the North Sea. The officers were each assigned a handsomely appointed state room by the boat's executive officer, Lt. Cdr. Vincent Astor. Astor himself was no stranger to luxury, having been acknowledged as the "richest young man in the world" upon inheriting $69 million when his father John Jacob Astor died on the *Titanic*. Astor had enlisted at the start of the war and also loaned his own magnificent yacht, *Noma*, to the navy.

The surrendered U-boats were moored in groups of six to eight boats in what the British called "trots." The American crews soon dubbed the entire U-boat compound the "trot." The United States had selected six U-boats as its prizes, representative samples from each of the different classes: the long-range U-cruiser, UB short-range coastal boats, and UC minelayers. The selected boats included U-117, U-140, U-164,

UB-88, UB-148, and UC-97. U-117 and U-140 would have added interest to the public, as they had operated off the U.S. coast in 1918. Combined, the six boats had sunk ninety-one vessels during the war, forty-one of them American.

The officers given command of these boats included lieutenant commanders Aquilla G. Dibrell (U-117), G. A. Hulings (U-140), Freeland A. Daubin (U-164), Joseph L. Nielson (UB-88), Harold T. Smith (UB-148), and Holbrook Gibson (UC-97). Charles Lockwood became executive officer of UC-97.

Commissioned less than a month before the end of the war, U-164 had been chosen because it represented the latest in submarine developments. However, when Lt. Cdr. Daubin pulled the assignment to command that boat and first stepped aboard, he was shocked at its condition. Souvenirs hunters had already struck, and the sub had been cannibalized for spare parts by the British, French, and Italians. As Daubin described it, "Had a depth charge been dropped down the main hatch, it couldn't have done greater damage." He estimated that he would need three or four months to get it in working order, time he did not have. While Daubin scrambled to find a suitable replacement, the other commanders set to work on their boats.

Lockwood and his skipper, Holbrook Gibson, set off with a tug and a dozen men, excited to take possession of their new ship. They found the Harwich estuary overflowing with U-boats; some 160 of them remained. The rusting hulks of the once proud U-boat fleet had clearly been neglected since their surrender in November. When they located UC-97, their hearts sank at its deteriorated condition.

Not knowing quite what they were working with, they began to cautiously charge batteries, throw switches, and open valves. Wartime shortages of lubricating oil had forced Germany to make compromises on engine cooling in small coastal boats as the UC-97. While testing the engines and charging batteries, the crew burned through several piston heads, forcing repeated repairs and a nighttime raid on other U-boats in the trot to scavenge spare pistons for the upcoming voyage to the United States

Lt. Cdr. J.L. Nielson took command of UB-88 on March 13, 1919. The U-boat had been surrendered on November 29 and since that date had received no attention. All of the officers and about half of the crew assigned to UB-88 had submarine experience. Their assignment was to clean and repair the boat, make it operational, train the crew, and sail for America under their own power as soon as possible. But the challenges were daunting.

The German crew had thrown food into the bilges, which now emitted a sickening stench. Souvenir hunters had stripped the magnetic compass and other instruments. Dents from depth charge attacks dimpled the deck. Condensation had rusted exposed metal surfaces in the engine room as well as on the torpedoes that lay scattered on the floor in the torpedo room. The batteries were dead and the engines rusted. Every piece of equipment had to be cleaned, repaired, or replaced. Crew members scavenged parts from other U-boats. The ship went into floating dry dock March 21–24 for inspection, painting, and repairs. Over a two-week period the boat was made operational and habitable and readied for its voyage.

In an inspired bit of naval horse trading, Lt. Cdr. Daubin swapped U-164 for U-111 and took his crew aboard to confront the bewildering complexity of a U-boat. Gaining technical understanding of the submarines would be a challenge. The American crew of U-111 confronted a wilderness of levers, valves, gauges, and wheels, labeled with obscure engineering terms that baffled even the crew members who spoke German.

"Kuhldruck" read the label above one valve. Now, what in blazes did that mean? They followed the pipe leading from the valve as it passed through a tangle of other pipes,

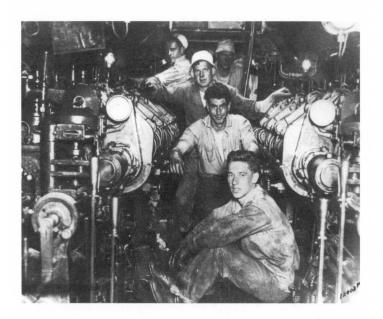

15. These American sailors worked in the gritty, claustrophobic confines of UB-88's engine room to repair the rusted parts of two four-cycle diesel engines and learn their operation in preparation for the voyage to America. Navy Historical Center photo courtesy Gary Fabian

over racks and beneath batteries and oxygen tanks, until they realized that it connected to the water cooling apparatus. They scribbled notes and diagrams of the lines for air, water, lubricating oil, and fuel, and the ventilating pipes, battery leads, and lighting circuits. Those who worked with engines, electrical systems, or ventilation put their piece of the puzzle together and linked it with the next component.

The biggest challenge arose when the U-111 crew realized that the main bearings on the starboard engine were burned out. The Germans had closed off the valves to the lubricating oil line just before surrendering the boat, allowing the engines to overheat. Working without the proper tools or equipment, in shifts round the clock, the engineers began improvising makeshift ways to get the job done. Still, when the other U.S. U-boats were ready to depart, U-111's one engine lay in pieces, and U-140 had no engines at all. U-111 would sail once it finished repairs. U-140 would eventually be towed across the Atlantic by a coal ship, but never participated in the bond campaign.

On April 3 the UB-88, UB-148, UC-97, and U-117, along with the submarine tender *Bushnell*, set a course for America along the long, calm southern route by way of the Azores and Bermuda. The group was given the unofficial name of the Ex-German Submarine Expeditionary Force. Because of ongoing engine repairs, UC-97 began the voyage being towed by *Bushnell*, but was soon under its own power. At 185 feet in length and 520 tons, UC-97 had been designed for short coastal missions, not arduous ocean voyages. The crew could coax no more than a lumbering nine knots from its engines. That set the speed for the entire group and raised concerns that the U-boats would not make it to New York in time for the opening of the bond drive on April 21.

Twice during the voyage, the group had to stop while *Bushnell* lowered a boat to transfer spare pistons to UC-97 for makeshift engine repairs. The commander of the force aboard the *Bushnell* finally signaled that if UC-97 could not make New York on its own, its crew should come aboard the *Bushnell*, and the U-boat would once again be taken in tow. This seemed too ignoble an end to the nearly-completed trans-ocean adventure of sailing the crippled enemy craft home. Commander Gibson declined the offer. His crew performed another makeshift engine repair miracle that allowed the U-boat to limp through the rest of the voyage.

When stormy weather kicked up, life became miserable. Aboard UB-88 all hatches remained closed as the boat pitched and rolled badly and took constant spray against the conning tower. The air inside became foul. At night, the running lights of the other submarines and the *Bushnell* would disappear for minutes at a time behind the waves, making it difficult to keep formation. In the officers' quarters on UB-88 they kept a track chart that recorded their daily noontime position. The chart showed very little progress against the foul weather.

On the ninth day out, UB-88 and U-117 received permission to leave the group and sail ahead on their own at a faster pace. They would shortly be met by two destroyers sent from New York to escort them. Cinematographers on the destroyers' decks filmed the exciting event of ex-German submarines piloted by U.S. sailors on their way to America. Such newsreels played in movie houses around the country.

A Diet of Pickles and Jelly

When U-111 was finally ready to leave Harwich on April 7, Captain Daubin realized that he would not be able to catch up with the other U-boats. Trailing behind them on the same southern route would likely cause the U-111 to be late for Victory Loan festivities planned in New York. His other option was to sail the speedier—but riskier—passage across the North Atlantic.

Because of concerns about the reliability of the boats and lack of training for the crews, it had been decided that all of the U-boats would make their voyage strictly on the surface. Daubin would be venturing on a route notorious for its bad weather in a vessel of uncertain seaworthiness. In addition, he would be on his own and without a functioning wireless radio and therefore unable to summon help if needed. Other Allied nations that had tried to sail U-boats home under their own power had all met with failure. The boats had foundered or been taken in tow. So being alone without wireless carried considerable risk.

Fogs, gales, and heavy seas troubled the boat all the way. Disaster nearly struck when an open seacock began filling the boat with water. But a crewman crawled into the slimy

16. Crewmen pose for reporters at the deck gun of U-111, newly arrived at the Brooklyn Navy Yard. Library of Congress

water beneath one of the massive diesel engines to close it off. In their haste to begin their voyage, the crew had not taken on enough provisions, forcing them to survive on pickles and jelly for the last few days of the voyage.

The repaired engine bearings held up until they reached Nantucket, where they lost the use of one of the two diesel engines. The boat limped into New York Harbor on April 19, days ahead of the other U-boats, flying the German naval standard on its mast below the Stars and Stripes.

By virtue of arriving first, it fell to U-111 to give the American public its first exposure to a German U-boat. Reporters who toured the boat reported about the pluck and ingenuity of the American crew. The concept of submarines was still very much a novelty that had to be communicated to a fascinated public. "Take a series of hat boxes and knock the bottoms out and take the covers off. Then join them together until you have, say, a dozen in line." This was one reporter's attempt to convey the strangeness of life aboard a U-boat.

17. The four surrendered U-boats that made the Atlantic crossing together are shown here shortly after their arrival at the Brooklyn Navy Yard in April 1919. Press photo from 1919, source unknown

"Smear the interior with grease as thick as possible. Cover the walls with gauges, pumps, little wheels and all the center spaces with machinery. In any odd corner place a few bunks."

After a twenty-three-day voyage, UB-88 and U-117 made port on April 26, and the other vessels of the Ex-German Submarine Expeditionary Force soon followed. New York's native son, Vincent Astor, piloted U-117 to its berth. The young heir to the Astor fortune had come home from the war. When Astor joined the navy in June 1917, he made the foolhardy boast that he would bring home a German submarine. Darned if he didn't do it. Reporters crowded round him as he stepped down the gangplank with his pet wirehaired terrier Jim. With his characteristic modesty, he praised the boat and the crew and then left for the more challenging peacetime assignment of managing his considerable investments.

The public did not yet have access to the boats, but swarms

18. A sawtooth blade crowned the bow of the U-boats for cutting through entrapping submarine nets deployed by the Allies. The American crew of UB-88 painted an eye on its bow to make the boat appear more ominous. Naval History and Heritage Command photo courtesy Gary Fabian

of official visitors descended on the submarines. Dozens of technicians from the navy, from shipyards that built submarines, and from companies that supplied equipment for submarines all showed up to give the vessels a thorough examination.

Allowed onto the boats in advance of the public, newspaper reporters obliged with stories that described the boats in language from the war: Sea Monsters, Hun Devil Boats, Sea Thugs, Undersea Dastards, and Slayer of Innocents. Newspaper coverage roused public interest in the role the U-boats would play in the Victory Bond drive and in upcoming exhibition cruises that two of the U-boats would soon undertake around the country.

Newspaper photographs of the U-boats gave the impression of armor-plated leviathans. A distinctive sawtooth blade angled off their bows. It had been designed to cut through entrapping submarine nets, but photographed from the right angle, it looked more like a row of menacing teeth. Photographs of the large deck guns, torpedo tubes, and the mine-laying apparatus conveyed the lethality of these warships. Although the information was not always accurate, articles also reported the U-boats' war records: how many ship they had sent to the bottom and whether they had operated off the U.S. coast.

The crews spent a very busy few days scrubbing and painting their boats. Given free rein to decorate the submarines, the crews adorned them with iron crosses, German coats of arms, and camouflage. Each boat was issued a regulation Imperial German Navy man-of-war flag to be flown under the U.S. flag in the traditional manner for designating a surrendered vessel. They were now ready to take center stage in a celebration of the end of the war.

5

SELLING BONDS

The visits of the captured Hun pirates, harmless and toylike
now, will do much to call the attention of the people to the
daring of our men who fought these underseas dastards and
the right they have to ask that we finally settle the bills of the
war and help the country to a peace basis.
—*The South Amboy (NJ) Citizen*, May 10, 1919

One of the posters for the Victory Loan campaign pictured a
weary, dejected American soldier sitting on a dock in France,
his duffel bag and a souvenir German helmet at his feet,
while ships sailed off in the background. "Bring him home
with the Liberty Loan," read the message. In the summer
of 1919, some five hundred thousand American soldiers still
waited in Europe for their return home. The transportation
service that had so miraculously conveyed vast armies to the
war zone the previous summer now shuttled back and forth
across the Atlantic moving them in the opposite direction.
Hostilities had ceased but not the costs of war.

As it had done four previous times during the war, the
government planned to help cover the cost through the
sale of bonds. The campaign was referred to as a "loan,"
since the government intended to borrow the money from
its citizens, for which privilege it would pay 4.75% interest,
convertible in three or four years, and exempt the earn-
ings from income tax. Previous campaigns went by the
name Liberty Loan, which now was changed to Victory
Loan. Loan officials expected to reach their $4.5 billion
goal within three weeks, but only if they pulled out all of

the stops and utilized everything they had learned in the previous loan drives.

Weapons and equipment had been popular attractions during the third Liberty Loan campaign in April 1918. Cannons and implements of trench warfare, mostly borrowed from the French, traveled throughout the country on war exhibit trains, accompanied by Liberty Loan orators and soldiers. The trains proved a huge success, introducing the war to the public as never before. For the fourth Liberty Loan later that year, exhibit trains offered the additional attraction of war trophies. Shiploads of German guns and helmets were brought home as quickly as they could be captured on the battlefield. They traveled the country along with U.S. Army items, and soldiers of Allied armies: French Foreign Legion, Belgian units with dog teams, Italian Alpine troops. During this last campaign, exhibit trains covered an estimated one hundred thousand miles, making four stops a day and attracting substantial crowds in communities large and small. Military airplanes entered the act by participating in flying circuses that took air shows to over eighty cities.

It was a simple but successful formula—displaying war matériel and weapons made people feel more connected to the war and more willing to support it with their hard-earned dollars. Officials planned to follow the same formula for the Victory Loan. In the run-up to the April 21 start of the Victory Loan campaign, three aerial circuses and thirty war exhibit trains began touring the country with speakers and exhibits. The army scheduled appearances by 220 tanks to support Loan events. New York, Chicago, Boston, and Philadelphia created "Victory Ways," public space to display war trophies and celebrate the battles in which American troops participated.

Expectations ran high for the ability of the U-boats to draw crowds and sell bonds. Victory Loan officials huddled

Every **LIBERTY BOND**
is a shot
at a **U BOAT**

FIRE *YOUR* SHOT
TO-DAY
BUY A
LIBERTY BOND

SECOND
LIBERTY
LOAN

19. The specter of the U-boat was used throughout the war to motivate the purchase of war bonds. Library of Congress

with the captains to outline their ambitious plans for the U-boats. They would first participate in the huge Victory Loan celebration in New York. Then, within the brief period of the bond drive, the U-boats would visit cities in the northeastern United States to support their Victory Loan events. Two of the boats, UC-97 and UB-88, would then strike out on extended exhibition tours to aid in bond drive celebrations, support navy recruitment drives, and show off these war trophies to nearly every coastal city in the United States.

UB-148 would make calls around New York, travel up the Hudson as far as possible, then go to Bridgeport and eventually layup at New London. U-111's schedule took it to Portland, then on to Portsmouth, Boston, New Bedford, Newport, Providence, and New Haven before laying up at New London. U-117 would head south to Philadelphia, Wilmington (Delaware), Wilmington (North Carolina), Norfolk, Baltimore, Annapolis, and Charleston, South Carolina,, then layup at Washington DC. UC-97's destination was the Great Lakes by way of the Saint Lawrence River, including several Canadian stops. And the most ambitious schedule fell to UB-88, which would visit cities along the Gulf of Mexico, the Mississippi River, and then travel through the Panama Canal to the West Coast.

To measure overall progress of the campaign, a "Victory Ship" set out from San Francisco on opening day headed for New York. Its speed throughout the campaign would be determined day to day by the nation's rate of bond purchases. To move the Victory Ship forward one mile required $857,142.85 in bond sales. As the campaign progressed, the ship would sail through the Panama Canal and work its way northward along the Atlantic Coast, and then—if things went as planned—bond sales would hit their $4.5 billion target on May 10, the last day of the campaign, and the ship would sail triumphantly into New York's "Victory Harbor."

As the campaign got under way, six thousand Victory Loan films opened in theaters throughout the nation, featuring movie stars urging their fans to buy bonds. Prominent companies and individuals led the local campaign drives with huge pledges. Businesses and organizations prided themselves on having 100 percent employee participation. Individual purchasers could proudly display their Victory Loan banner or pin as a mark of having done their patriotic duty.

The keen spirit of competition further stirred participation. Each Federal Reserve District had its quota, as did each state, county, city, town, and Victory Loan official. Progress reports poured into the Treasury Department, and newspapers monitored the daily tally. In the opening days of the campaign, forty-four towns in New England exceeded their quota. Twelve counties in the Atlanta district blew past their goal. The state of Oklahoma led in its Reserve district. Some communities in northern Ohio doubled their quota from the last campaign. These newspaper reports created the impression that everyone was rising to the challenge and anyone not giving maximum effort would be counted a slacker.

Battle Week Launches Bond Drive in New York

The deck of UC-97 bristled with Victory Loan officials on April 29 as it led the flotilla of the U-boats from the Brooklyn Navy Yard to the battery. Cdr. Charles Lockwood, operating the boat from the conning tower, turned to the woman beside him and asked if she wanted to steer the submarine. By her very presence, Mrs. John T. Pratt had already become the first American woman ever to ride on a U-boat. Now she took the helm and became the first to ever pilot a German submarine. The wife of a Brooklyn oil magnate, Mrs. Pratt headed up the Women's Committee for the Victory Loan. She would tell the newspapers that piloting UC-97 was the most exciting moment of her life.

UC-97 came to shore first, leading UB-88, UB-148, and U-117. The band from the battleship *North Dakota* struck up a lusty medley while airplanes and a blimp circled overhead. This was the first public showing of the U-boats, and a large crowd had gathered for a ceremony to dedicate them to the Victory Loan campaign. They pressed forward with somber curiosity for a closer look.

Few trophies of the war populated so many nightmares as did the U-boat, an understanding not lost on the small army of Victory Loan workers who circulated through the crowd, exhorting sales. "Suppose the German flag were on those boats now," one called out. "You're going to buy bonds, aren't you?" And they did. Reporters suggested that the crowd's thoughts stirred with still-fresh memories of the evil deeds of U-boats and the many souls lost at sea. And with the *Lusitania*. Always the *Lusitania*.

With the U-boats as backdrop, a number of speakers discussed the role of the navy in the war. Over the next twelve days, these enemy submarines would go on public display in dozens of cities, providing tangible proof of the navy's success in ridding the seas of these pirates. Through a telephone and loudspeaker hookup from Washington, DC, the assistant secretary of the navy, Franklin Roosevelt, added his thoughts on the importance of participation in the Victory Loan.

Following the ceremony the four U-boats sailed up the Hudson, accompanied by twelve sub chasers. The nimble sub chasers showed off the bursts of speed they had used to help contain the U-boat threat to America's shores. Twelve battleships of the Atlantic Fleet had been anchored in the Hudson for over a week receiving thousands of visitors. As the U-boats cruised past those battleships first in line—*Mississippi, Nevada, Oklahoma*—sailors crowded the railings for a view, and ships' bands began to play. Though it had been the primary focus of their wartime efforts, few of these sailors had actually seen the elusive U-boat, and they were as curious as the average civilian. The scene repeated itself all the way through the fleet until the submarines tied up at 79th Street, where they would be on public display.

While the navy's involvement in Battle Week unfolded on the Hudson, the army celebrated throughout the city. Displays of war trophies transformed Park Avenue into "Victory Way." Artillery, trench mortars, machine guns, and a giant pyramid of captured German spike helmets represented the spoils from fighting at Château-Thierry, Saint Mihiel, the Argonne Forest, and other engagements in which U.S. soldiers participated. In Times Square, the "Argonne Forest Theatre" recreated that battle landscape with gnarled underbrush and shell-blasted trees in order to celebrate the role of the famous "lost battalion," which had been part of New York City's own 77th Division.

Every day a packed schedule of events enticed the public onto the streets for pageants, drills, displays, parades, seaplane races, and concerts. The king of patriotic marches, John Philip Sousa, conducted the massed bands of the Atlantic fleet. It was impossible to attend any of these activities

20. During its month-long stay in Washington DC, U-117 received a steady stream of visitors, including government and military officials. Here the curious public packs the deck to capacity. Courtesy Gary Fabian

without passing by one of the seventy-six bond sales booths set up to remind citizens of their patriotic duty.

U-Boats Sell Bonds

As the month of May began, Victory Loan officials at the Treasury Department had cause to worry. By this date, half way into the campaign, they had met only one quarter of their $4.5 billion goal. The Victory Loan ship USS *Marblehead* had steamed briskly on the first leg of the voyage from San Francisco to San Diego, matching its speed to the initial surge of bond subscriptions. At San Francisco, the destroyer *Crane* took up the Victory Ship relay, but sales had fallen off and did not warrant her top speed of thirty-five knots. Several times *Crane* issued an SOS to communities across the nation, urging citizens to buy more bonds to keep the ship on a pace to reach New York by the close of the campaign on May 10.

21. This crowd of visitors, curious about U-117 when it stopped at Norfolk VA in May 1919, was typical of the enthusiastic reception all of the surrendered U-boats received when they visited coastal cities to sell bonds during Victory Loan campaign. Original photo from the author's collection

The U-boats took up the challenge, fanning out along the East Coast to promote sales. While UC-97 remained at New York for that city's continuing Victory Loan celebrations, UB-148 began its schedule in Hoboken and Jersey City. U-117 headed for Philadelphia and Washington DC, while UB-88 struck out on its long exhibition cruise of the Gulf Coast, the Mississippi River, and the West Coast. UB-88 would have only one scheduled stop during the bond campaign, at Savannah.

Under repair at the Brooklyn Navy Yard, U-111 had missed the ceremony at the battery. Now it set out for New England, first to Portland and Portsmouth, then to Boston. No area of the country had as extensive a connection to submarines in general and U-boats in particular as New England. The pre-war visits of the German submarines *Deutschland* and U-53 to New London and Newport awakened America to the long-range capabilities of German submarines and their lethality. The New England coast had been hit especially hard by U-boat attacks in 1918. The navy's first submarine base opened in New London during the war, and the two shipbuilding yards that constructed U.S. submarines were also located in New England.

On May 1, when U-111 sailed up Boston's Charles River to the Boston Basin, loaded with exuberant Victory Loan officials, interest in the visitor could not have been higher. At 240 feet in length and eight hundred tons displacement, it was larger than America's wartime submarines, but similar in displacement to the latest S-class submarines being developed. Two 2,400 horsepower diesel engines could power U-111 to nineteen knots on the surface, while electric motors pushed it to ten knots while submerged. Naval officers said the U-boat was built more along the lines of a destroyer than a submarine. The two guns mounted on its deck bore out that comparison.

Mistaken newspaper reports that U-111 was one of the U-boats that terrorized the New England coast in 1918 swelled the crowd of onlookers lining the route from Boston's harbor to the basin. Those who wanted to make a closer inspection would have to purchase a bond to do so. Within a couple hours of U-111 mooring, campaign officials in the area sold out of bonds and had to call for more.

Still, bond sales in Boston and the New England district lagged. To reach their quota by the May 10 deadline, New England citizens would have to subscribe to the loan at a rate of $25 million a day. Boston had erected a huge public board to show the progress of the Victory Ship. By now the ship should have been passing through the Panama Canal,

22. The scene looks tranquil as visitors examine U-111 in
Boston. However, the U-boat's visit coincided with a riot
of marchers sympathetic to Russia's Bolshevik revolution.
Boston Public Library, Leslie Jones Collection

but slow bond sales had it cruising at a leisurely pace along
the Baja Peninsula.

The campaign needed all the help it could get. The battleship *Kentucky* made port calls along the New England
coast. While U-111 welcomed visitors in Boston, the city also
hosted an artillery train. On a month-long tour of the country, the train comprised seventeen cars loaded with thirty
pieces of artillery and other military equipment. A military band led the procession of cannons, trench mortars,
anti-aircraft guns, and eight-inch howitzers through the
business district, attracting large crowds. Individual guns
were exhibited at prominent locations, along with other war
gear, such as a thirty-six-inch spotlight, a field radio out-
fit, ambulance, and a carrier pigeon vehicle. Fifteen of the
heavy guns went on display on Boston Commons, mak-

ing frequent firings that reverberated throughout the city. Across town, Will Rogers and Eddie Cantor exhorted the audience at the Colonial Theater to subscribe to the loan. Al Jolson auctioned off bonds at the Boston Opera House.

Although the patriotically charged frenzy of the Victory Loan gave no indication, the nation's attention had already begun to shift away from supporting the war to dealing with its aftermath. With only these final bills to pay through the Victory Loan and the whole bitter business of peace to sort out at Versailles, America could resume its march to primacy in the world. Except that the war had changed that vision for many.

On the day U-111 opened for inspection in Boston, a crowd filed from the Dudley Street Opera House in the Roxbury neighborhood and moved as a mass along the street. Instead of heading over to the basin to see U-111, they unfurled red flags and handed out Bolshevik literature. They had just attended a May Day meeting, which had fired them with the causes of socialism and labor reform.

It was fortunate that the Victory Loan campaign was so short, for the national attention span could not have sustained it much longer. In the benumbed aftermath of the war, political unrest had quickly moved to center stage. Amid riots, bomb attacks against public figures, a wave of labor strikes, and mounting anxiety over the spreading Bolshevik Revolution, public hostility turned from the old enemy of Germany to the new enemy of radicalism. Bolsheviks, socialists, anarchists, and labor organizers were stealing the public stage away from war bonds and U-boats and emerging as the new focus of public hostility.

When the Roxbury marchers ignored police orders to disperse, an all-out brawl ensued. Shots dropped three policemen. Even with police reinforcements, the marchers kept the upper hand until soldiers, sailors, and civilians rushed in to assist the police. For several minutes a serious street

23. U-111 in Boston flies the Stars and Stripes above the
German naval standard in the traditional display for
a surrendered vessel. Boston Public Library,
Leslie Jones Collection

battle raged with guns, knives, and fists. Police eventually
carted 112 people off to prison.

In the final months of the war, Socialist rebellions had
erupted in the German navy. Mutinous sailors took control of naval bases at Kiel and Wilhelmshaven. When time
came to surrender the German fleet and its U-boats, suffi-

cient crews could barely be mustered that would still obey their officers. Even now, America's "Polar Bear Division," along with Allied troops, battled revolutionary forces in Arctic Russia, near Archangel. Now it seemed the contagion had followed the U-boats to America.

"Bolsheviki are right here in our midst in very large numbers," Boston's district attorney sounded the alarm in the newspaper. "Right here in Boston and throughout the country." No one disputed his claim. Similar May Day riots had broken out in New York, Cleveland, Denver, and other cities.

Let's Have a Closer Look at That Sub

Despite the distraction of riots, U-111 sold $80,000 in bonds during its three-day stay in Boston. Everywhere the U-boats visited, they achieved great success at stimulating bond sales. But the boats had also excited keen interest from the small group of companies and navy engineering bureaus devoted to building the navy's next generation of submarines. The stated goals for bringing the U-boats to America may have been to sell bonds, but the navy's motivation had been to learn about German submarine technology.

When U-111 departed Boston on May 4, heading for New Bedford, it carried Victory Loan officials plus seven employees of the Fore River Ship and Engine Building Company come down from their facility in Quincy to check out this marvel of German engineering. Working for the Electric Boat Company, Fore River was one of only two contractors that built submarines for the U.S. Navy. The U.S. submarine R-8 had launched at Fore River only two weeks ago. A month before the end of the war, Fore River also built submarine S-1, the first of the navy's new generation of S-class submarines. S-2, launched in February of that year (1919), had been constructed by the only other company building U.S. submarines, the Lake Torpedo Company of Bridgeport, Connecticut.

The progression of U.S. submarine development was

sometimes characterized as an alphabet soup of submarine types. When war broke out in Europe in July 1914, the U.S. Navy boasted six submarines in its fleet, four A-boats and two B-boats. By the end of 1915, fifty-nine were in operation or under construction, in various classes from A to N, each an improvement on its predecessor.

Reports from the initial testing of the surrendered U-boats in England and the navy's experience with the boats since taking possession of its allotment were glowingly praiseworthy. The U-boats were durable vessels, powered by reliable diesel engines, with superior ventilation and navigation systems, and quality optics beyond anything available in America. They could operate at sea for months at a time, thousands of miles from their base. This stood them in marked contrast to U.S. submarines, which had been plagued with a variety of design and engineering problems and had been built largely for short-range coastal defense. Commander Lockwood, who had helped to sail UC-97 across the Atlantic and would later become its skipper, acknowledged in his post-war memoir, *Down to the Sea in Subs*, that "We had much to learn from these enemy boats."

The navy was quick to point out that its new S-class submarines had a higher speed and a longer cruising range. The latest U.S. submarine, S-3, could also claim better habitability and seaworthiness. Over the coming months and years, various themes played out in the U-boat vs. U.S. submarine scenario. Although continuing examination of the U-boats confirmed their superiority, the message for public consumption was that America's S-class submarines now being built were overall better vessels.

But for six more days at least, focus remained squarely on motivating the American public to finish paying for the war. Matching its speed to the rate of sales, the Victory ship *Crane* completed its passage through the Panama Canal to the accompaniment of screeching whistles and flag salutes along the entire waterway. The destroyer *Calhoun* took up the relay from there and pointed its bow toward New York.

A suffocating Cape Cod fog enveloped U-111 as it made its way to New Bedford, the next destination on its tight schedule of visits, forcing it to wait out the foggy night at anchor. The following day, when it finally arrived at New Bedford, the Victory Loan committee gave it the cold shoulder. The U-boat had already stayed over in Boston for an extra day and then spent another day stranded in fog, but no one had thought to send word to New Bedford. A banquet had been arranged, hotel accommodations made, and a pilot sent out to escort the submarine to port. The New Bedford Loan Committee was not in a cooperative mood when the U-boat arrived for an abbreviated visit.

To further exacerbate the situation, the New Bedford loan committee had told residents that anyone who purchased a bond would qualify to tour the submarine. Eager residents showed up at the pier wearing the pins they received for a bond purchase to learn that only those who actually purchased a bond *on* the U-boat would get a tour. The newspaper reported that several boys, proudly wearing their bond pins, watched crestfallen from dockside, having been denied a tour. U-111 made a quick departure for Newport.

The Victory Ship *Calhoun* had arrived in the Gulf of Mexico. The recent uptick in subscriptions forced it to put on full speed of thirty-five knots for the first time since the trip began. However, reaching the target by the May 10 close of the campaign was still very much in question. Going into the final days of the drive, the nation had met only 62 percent of the goal. St. Louis and Minneapolis stood at one and two for the highest percentage of quota reached. New York had jumped from fifth to third. The *New York Times* reported the progress of trade groups at reaching their goal. The Allied Music Trades led the list on May 5, having raised $7 million, 254 percent of their quota, whereas art dealers lagged far behind with a meager 14 percent. The city itself, which stood at only 41 percent of its goal as the campaign entered its final week, kicked things into high gear.

Thousands of police and firemen circulated on the streets with persistent appeals to everyone. During the day airplanes towed messages to "Buy Victory Notes," and at night giant searchlights illuminated the sky. Generals, admirals, statesmen, soldiers, sailors, and pretty girls spoke at public rallies in support of the campaign. Speakers asked everyone to look on his neighbor's lapel or waistband for the symbol of their true patriotism, the button that showed they had subscribed to the loan.

In the final four days, the addition of a red feather marked those who had not only subscribed for what they thought they could afford, but who had dug still deeper and subscribed again. People could not take a walk without some banker, businessman, or enthusiastic volunteer exhorting them from booths on the street, while door-to-door appeals targeted homes and businesses.

On May 6, the Seventy-seventh Division, conscripted from New York City and surrounding areas, paraded up Fifth Avenue from Washington Square to 110th Street. Led by a cortege to honor the dead, twenty-seven thousand soldiers marched by battalions, each stretching for a city block, from curb to curb, moving in olive drab lockstep with fixed bayonets. The *New York Times* thought they looked "thick standing as a field of wheat." The Seventy-seventh had been the first drafted division to reach Europe and took ten thousand casualties during fighting at Château-Thierry, Meuse-Argonne, and Oise-Aisne. The sight of their proud return to the city inspired the one million spectators along the route to buy more bonds.

Commemorating the *Lusitania*

UC-97 cast off from its East Twenty-Third Street berth and eased into the East River around noon on May 7, 1919. As the Victory Loan entered its final days, the U-boat had been given the duty of marking a solemn anniversary in the Great War. Four years earlier, on this day, at this hour, the Cunard Line shipping company in New York received first word from its Liverpool office of a disaster at sea. "The *Lusitania*, we regret to advise, an unconfirmed report states to have been torpedoed by a submarine at 2 P.M. Friday, ten miles from Kinsale, and sunk at 2:30. There is no news as to the safety of passengers and crew."

The grand passenger liner *Lusitania*, traveling from America, had been torpedoed by a U-boat, with the loss of 1,198 lives, including 128 Americans. Universal outrage and revulsion exploded in newspaper editorials the following day. The attack was murder, plain and simple. German submarines operated in defiance of every principle of international law and common humanity.

Next to the mass slaughter unfolding on the battlefields of France, the sinking of the *Lusitania* barely registered on the scale of military horror. But it represented America's first real introduction to total war, a brand of war fought as much against civilians, including women and children, as against soldiers. Newspapers gave extensive coverage to the tragedy, with photos of bedraggled survivors, beached life boats, and coffins piled in mass graves. No other single event so firmly established the U-boat in the public imagination as an object of fear and revulsion and turned public opinion decisively against the German cause.

UC-97 cruised past the tip of Manhattan and rounded Governor's Island, there picking up the same route that the ill-fated passenger liner took as it departed New York Harbor in 1915. By the time the U-boat passed into the lower bay and headed for open ocean, a parallel activity began to unfold at the Cathedral of St. John the Divine in Morningside Heights, a few blocks north of Pier 54 where *Lusitania* had last docked. Five hundred people crowded the church by 4:30 p.m., the exact time when official news of the torpedoing of the great ship first reached New York.

"Through the martyrs of the *Lusitania*," Dr. Charles Lewis Slattery observed in his sermon, "our people were joined in a new faith with the suffering peoples of Europe." If the free nations had purchased the world's freedom without America's involvement, Slattery imagined, "we would have been in a moral position far worse than I care to fancy."

Even as Dr. Slattery saluted the *Lusitania* martyrs, UC-97 bobbed in choppy waves three miles off Sandy Hook, New Jersey, near the mouth of the Ambrose Channel, the point at which *Lusitania* would have set its course across the Atlantic. UC-97 carried on its deck a large wreath of laurel, woodbine, and fern bound with a purple ribbon, inscribed, "In Memoriam *Lusitania*."

The skipper issued the command, and up went the church flag, the Stars and Stripes, and below it the German ensign. The crew assembled in a semicircle on deck behind the wreath and removed their hats as a bugler sounded "Taps." With the last note, the wreath slipped into the sea. The crew returned to their posts, and the U-boat headed back to the city. A reporter watching from a nearby press boat concluded, "Silent as her sister ship after her murderous deed of May 7, 1915, the UC-97 stole away."

On the day of the *Lusitania* ceremony on this side of the Atlantic, representatives of the Allied governments meeting in Versailles, France, handed over to the German representatives the terms of the treaty meant to bring official end to the war. The conditions were extraordinarily harsh. Germany had to acknowledge that the war was a crime and that it was responsible for all the loss and damage inflicted upon Allied governments, and a price in reparations was fixed on these damages.

Since Germany would also acknowledge offenses against "international morality," it would be required to hand over for military trial persons accused of "committing acts in violation of the laws and customs of war." Beyond that the terms greatly curtailed the German military. Germany would lose its navy and be limited to six battleships, six light cruisers, twelve torpedo boats, and no submarines. This document had to assure, as President Wilson put it, that "this agony shall not be gone through with again."

Many found deep satisfaction that this verdict came down on the very anniversary of the sinking of the *Lusitania*, which was widely seen as the greatest crime of the U-boat war. The treaty meted out some measure of justice, requiring compensation for shipping losses from U-boats and punishment for U-boat captains responsible for war crimes. A British mine had already exacted the ultimate justice from Walther Schwieger, the captain of the submarine that torpedoed *Lusitania*, when it sank his U-boat in 1917. However, most of the other U-boat captains in question had already disappeared. In the postwar years, Allied governments would push for the trial of those who planned and conducted Germany's submarine war.

UB-88 Begins Its Epic Cruise

Until this point, only cities in the northeast had the opportunity to see the vaunted U-boats. But the navy planned two exhibition cruises that would unfold at the conclusion of the Victory Loan campaign. UC-97 would sail down the St. Lawrence and into the Great Lakes. UB-88 would spend the summer visiting every major port on the Gulf Coast, the Mississippi River up to St. Louis, and then pass through the Panama Canal to reach West Coast cities as far north as Bremerton, Washington. The two U-boats would not be selling Victory Bonds at that point, but aiding navy recruitment and displaying the war trophies.

All during the opening frenzy of the loan campaign, UB-88 had remained at the Brooklyn Navy Yard preparing for its long exhibition cruise to the West Coast. Finally on May 5 it headed out with the submarine tender USCG *Tuscarora*. Of the forty-plus cities it planned to visit on the voyage, only the first—Savannah—fell before the close of the Victory Loan campaign. Savannah would serve as a trial run for the UB-88 crew to perfect the procedures of exhibiting a submarine.

Word went out to the mayor of Savannah with the date of UB-88's arrival and a request that he publicize the visit. When the submarine headed up the Savannah River on May 8, the crew learned just how popular an attraction the U-boat would be. At all of the buildings lining the river, people crowded at windows for a view of the historic visitor. Dock workers, stevedores loading ships, and people along the waterway paused to take in the sight and wave. Factories and ships gave a three-blast salute with their steam whistles.

As soon as UB-88 moored at the municipal dock, thousands of people flocked to the scene. Gangplanks positioned fore and aft allowed visitors to enter in one hatch, get a quick tour, and exit through the other. By stationing a crew member in each compartment of the vessel to answer questions and keep the visitors moving, the crew determined that they could accommodate about five thousand visitors a day.

Twenty-four Hours to Raise $1.2 Billion

One day prior to the Victory Loan campaign deadline, the Treasury Department announced that the country had so far met only 73 percent of the campaign goal, leaving only twenty-four hours to sell $1.2 billion in bonds.

Bridgeport, Connecticut counted on UB-148 to push it over the top of its Loan goal. However, when the U-boat reached the city for the final day of the campaign, the news of its arrival got pushed lower on the front page of the *Bridgeport Standard Telegram* by an article on the attempt by navy fliers to make the first transatlantic flight. The navy's giant hydroplanes that would attempt this epic crossing had made their way to Nova Scotia, their final jumping-off point. Bad weather, faulty equipment, flying accidents, and the efforts of competing teams of flyers had kept the nation's rapt attention for weeks.

Along with submarines, airplanes were another revolutionary technology to come of age during the war. To their advocates, both had the potential to change the nature of warfare, and both played their role in the Victory Loan campaign. While U-boats stirred up sales in coastal cities, the army's Air Service organized the Victory Loan Flying Circus, the "greatest flying program the United States has yet witnessed." Each of the three separate circuses on tour contained eighteen airplanes, including captured German Fokkers as well as the aircraft that served the Allied cause— SPADS SE-5s, and Curtiss-HS flying boats.

On a thirty day tour, running from April 10 to May 10, the circuses covered more than nineteen thousand miles in one-night stands, visiting eighty-eight cities in forty-five states. During performances, the large Curtis seaplanes attacked towns with pasteboard bombs containing Victory Loan pamphlets until German Fokkers swooped from the sky to attack them. To the delight of the watching crowds, the French Spads and British SE-5s came to the rescue, vanquishing the Fokkers in a lively aerial dog fight. Victory Loan speeches filled out the agenda. At each location, the individuals who subscribed the largest amounts to the loan got a ride in an army plane.

Atlantic flights and vanquished Fokkers did not detract from UB-148's arrival in Bridgeport. When it docked at eleven o'clock in the evening for that city's final campaign push, a cluster of newsmen waited to greet it, along with one enthusiastic citizen who bought a $5,000 bond on the spot. Bridgeport was a submarine town, home to the Lake

Torpedo Boat Company. Company founder Simon Lake had been inspired to build submarines after reading Jules Verne's 1870 novel *Twenty Thousand Leagues Under the Sea*. During the war, large crowds of local residents gathered on Long Island Sound to watch each time the company launched a new submarine. The UB-148 was a marvel of submarine construction, the crew told reporters as they toured the boat. However, it did not begin to measure up to the new submersible boats being built in this country, such as the Lake-built submarine berthed nearby. Bridgeport met its campaign goal during UB-148's visit.

The Final Day

The Victory Ship *Calhoun* arrived off Sandy Hook, New Jersey at noon on May 10 and anchored there awaiting official word that the Victory Loan had achieved its $4.5 billion goal. The plan was to steam into New York Harbor—"Victory Harbor"—at the precise hour when the country met the bond target. Orders came at three o'clock telling the ship to enter the harbor. The campaign had reached its goal.

U-boat UC-97 received the honor of escorting *Calhoun* on this concluding leg of its journey. When the two vessels passed the anchored battleship *Kentucky*, it boomed a twenty-one-gun salute that resonated throughout the city. A convoy of destroyers greeted the vessels at the Statue of Liberty and took the *Calhoun* to its berth. From there a Victory letter was dispatched from the mayor of San Francisco to the mayor of New York, bringing final close to the Victory Loan. From the beginning of the campaign to the end, the surrendered U-boats had played a key role in helping to pay the final cost of the conflict in which they had played such an important and infamous role.

6

THE FIRST SUBMARINE ON THE GREAT LAKES

As soon as word flashed that the sub was entering the harbor,
a wild scramble for places of vantage ensued, everybody in
Sandusky apparently wanting to see the "baby-killer" dock.
—*Sandusky (OH) Star-Journal*, June 23, 1919

UC-97's path to the Great Lakes lay through the St. Lawrence River and its system of Canadian locks and canals followed by a transit of the Welland Canal that bypassed Niagara Falls to enter Lake Erie. Halifax, Nova Scotia, served as the entry point. UC-97 arrived there on May 16, accompanied by the submarine tender *Bushnell*. Escort duty for the next leg of the trip would be handed over to the naval tug *Iroquois*.

No other Canadian city had as deep a connection to German submarines as Halifax, or to the war itself for that matter. When U-boats attacked the Canadian fishing fleet on the Grand Banks in 1918, the skies over Halifax and other Nova Scotia ports filled with flying boats, dirigibles, and kite balloons scouting for German submarines. Aside from the fishing fleet, Halifax also had considerable shipping to protect. The city served as transit point for Canadian troops and materials shipped off to war, carried by a steady stream of Canadian vessels.

Halifax gained tragic notoriety on December 6, 1917, when the explosive-laden cargo ship SS *Mont-Blanc* collided with another vessel in the harbor, unleashing a monstrous explosion that leveled nearly two square kilometers and killed two thousand people. The evidence of that tragedy could still be seen in the spring of 1919 when UC-97 made port, although the city was in the midst of a massive rebuilding effort. Most of the shipping traffic had now turned in the opposite direction as Canadian troops trickled home from Europe.

But the Canadian wound that still festered from the U-boat war went by the name *Llandovery Castle*. During the war, the Canadian government chartered the *Llandovery Castle* as a hospital ship to bring wounded soldiers home from England to Halifax. On June 27, 1918, U-86 torpedoed *Llandovery Castle* off the Irish coast, with a loss of 234 lives. It had been on a return trip to England, carrying a crew and medical staff. Under international law U-boats were permitted to stop hospital ships to determine whether they also carried troops or war matériel, which were not permitted. But U-boats could not sink hospital ships in the performance of their duties.

U-86 captain Helmut Patzig worked in reverse order, first sinking the ship and then determining from survivors in lifeboats if there had been any rationale for his actions. Learning that there had not been, Patzig took steps to conceal his crime. He first sent all his crew below deck except for a few officers, and then he opened fire on the lifeboats with his deck gun to eliminate witnesses. Last, Patzig swore his crew to secrecy and altered his log book to erase evidence of the attack. One lifeboat with twenty-four passengers survived to bring back word of the tragedy. It would enter into the history of this bloody war as the starkest example of the inhumanity of unrestricted submarine warfare.

Though the sinking of a hospital ship was callous, it had become commonplace. U-boats sank eleven hospital ships before the *Llandovery Castle*. However, on this occasion, international outrage focused on the killing of the survivors. Fourteen Canadian nursing sisters perished in the attack, and they figured prominently in the post-attack publicity. Posters and newspaper illustrations showed terrified nurses clinging to shattered lifeboats while being gunned by the U-boat or their lifeless bodies drifting underwater. *Llandovery Castle* had sailed from Halifax, and its crew included many from that city.

May I Introduce You to the U-Boat?

A newspaper wire story about UC-97's itinerary went out from Halifax, confirming the schedule of visits along the route. The U-boat would stop for one day in smaller communities and two days in major cities. Quebec and Montreal came first on the route, beginning May 23. During the first week of June, there would be stops at New York towns on Lake Ontario. Visits at Toronto and Hamilton, Ontario would follow. From there the Welland Canal would take UC-97 to Lake Erie and Buffalo. Detroit would host the popular war trophy for a July Fourth celebration, and Chicago would be its final destination. Wrapped around those destinations lay an ambitious schedule of visits to all cities on the Great Lakes.

With dates now set, towns and cities along the route made plans for the U-boat's visit. Naval recruiting offices scheduled events to capitalize on the expected excitement to be generated by having an enemy submarine in port. Towns formed committees to organize activities around the visit. Agendas got populated with banquets, speaking engagements, patriotic celebrations, band concerts, parades, and the arrival home of troops. A few towns not included for a stop contacted the Navy Department or their congressman to plead to be added to the schedule.

No one has ever stopped to calculate the number of column inches of newspaper articles devoted to submarines during the Great War. The number would be in the stratosphere. But it is safe to say that no movie star has ever approached that amount of publicity, and no advertising campaign better established a product in the public consciousness. In addition to continuous wartime news about U-boats, Hollywood stoked anti-German sentiment with such movies as *The Sinking of the Lusitania* (1918), a twelve-minute animated documentary. During 1919, as the surrendered U-boats toured American cities, movie producers and book publishers helped to publicize German submarines by continuing to work the U-boat theme.

The naval war served as the focus for a popular series of boys' books by writer Halsey Davidson, beginning in 1918 with *The Navy Boys After Submarines, or Protecting the Giant Convoys*. The conflict may have ended that year but not the appetite of boys for the high seas adventure of the submarine war. Davidson published four additional titles in 1919, including *The Navy Boys to the Rescue, or Answering the Wireless Call for Help* and *The Navy Boys Behind the Big Guns, or Sinking the German U-boats*. "Much is being written about the army and the aviation corps," one reviewer explained about *Big Guns*, "but little is said about the absorbing work now being done by Uncle Sam's Jackies [bluejackets or sailors]. Here we have a record of big gun work in helping to rid the ocean of the U-boat menace."

Four U-boat movies in 1919 also helped to keep the U-boat war fresh in the public mind. As with all of the wartime films, they offered no subtlety of characterization. Patriots were always in the right and victorious, and the Germans always behaved reprehensibly and deserved their horrible fate. In *Behind the Door*, one of the most gruesome of the U-boat movies, Wallace Beery plays a naval officer whose new bride is captured and killed by a U-boat crew. Beery captures the U-boat captain and takes bloody revenge.

Newspaper photos and movies aside, virtually no one living along the Great Lakes in 1919 had ever seen a submarine, let alone a German submarine, and yet the U-boat existed in their imagination as an alien marvel of modern engineering put to diabolical use. "Jules Verne never dreamed of such a mass of dials, gauges, and wheels," a reporter for the *Illustrated Buffalo Express* noted after touring UC-97.

As U-boats went, UC-97 was smaller than most. Its surface displacement of 491 tons, made it inferior in size to most U.S. submarines. On the whole a very average submersible—185 feet long, a beam of 18 feet 9 inches, and a draft of 12 feet 6 inches, capable of traveling at a leisurely speed of eleven knots on the surface and six knots submerged. And yet armed with three torpedo tubes, a 3.4-inch gun, and fourteen mines, it had ample capacity to sow destruction.

Although later evidence would reveal that UC-97 had been commissioned too late in the war to have seen action, at this point it was officially credited with having sunk seven Allied ships and taken fifty lives. Reporters along the route embellished its reputation or fused it with the worst horrors of submarine warfare. When the United States entered the war, President Wilson created the Committee on Public Information (CPI) as America's propaganda arm to control the news and mold it to support the war effort. For the CPI, truth was often subordinated to the larger purpose of shaping public opinion. In that same vein, reporters made UC-97 a stand-in for everything good and evil associated with U-boats.

The vicious reputation of U-boats, combined with the sheer beguiling physical appearance of UC-97, made for powerful symbolism for anyone who watched it drift silently into port or was fortunate enough to tour the vessel. UC-97 and its companion U-boat UB-88 served as blank slates onto which everyone wrote their own narrative: the evil enemy, the vanquished foe, a new generation of military weapon, superior technology that the United States had now surpassed, a siren call to adventure for young men.

Who could pass up this once-in-a-lifetime chance to see a piece of history?

UC-97 began its tour in the final week of May with stops at Quebec and Montreal, these visits coinciding with Canada's own Victory Bond campaign. The crew gained hands-on experience in the business of being a traveling tourist attraction. They stationed crew members strategically throughout the vessel to avoid accidents, overcome the reluctance of some female visitors to squeeze through tight hatches, and respond appropriately when guests complimented them on speaking such good English for a German.

A minor flap erupted in Montreal when the harbor master informed the UC-97's officers that they had to fly the Union Jack while in Canadian waters. The UC-97 refused to do so, explaining that merchant ships were required to do so when they entered a foreign port, but not warships. UC-97's mast flew the U.S. flag above the German flag as the traditional sign of a surrendered vessel, according to international custom.

The rift sparked protests at other Canadian stops, until Secretary Daniels felt obliged to write a letter to the editor of the *Toronto Star* to lay the matter to rest with the explanation that UC-97, as a commissioned ship in the U.S. Navy, was not required to fly foreign flags. The matter only served as additional publicity for the tour.

In Lake Ontario, the submarine swung south to the New York shore, first stopping at Ogdensburg, then at five other communities, attracting large crowds at each stop. Sailing toward Oswego, the crew was once again bedeviled by engine problems when one of its diesels broke down, and the *Iroquois* had to take the sub in tow. But the crew had become masters at stopgap engine repairs and quickly had the problem fixed. The *Oswego Daily Times* reported that many people came from surrounding communities to see and tour the submarine.

Join the Navy and See the World

The role the U-boat would play on the rest of its voyage came into sharp focus in Oswego. It began with a change of skippers. Captain Gibson received orders transferring him to the Philadelphia Navy Yard, where he would oversee a technical evaluation of several of the surrendered U-boats. This would place him at the center of the U-boat vs. U.S. submarine controversy that would smolder well into the 1920s.

Charles Lockwood UC-97's executive officer became its new skipper. A navy recruiting team from New York joined the UC-97 victory tour in Oswego, coming aboard the accompanying tug boat for the rest of the cruise. From here on, the U-boat would be visiting dozens of American cities where the enemy submarine would attract young men like a magnet, offering perfect opportunities to sign up new recruits.

The recruiters traveling with UC-97 planned to set up shop on the deck of the submarine, sign young men into the navy on the spot, and then take them right aboard the tug and deliver them to the Great Lakes Naval Station near Chicago to begin training.

When the U-boat sailed back across Lake Ontario to visit more Canadian cities, it became clear that not only was the boat a magnet for young men, but also for politicians. Sailing into Toronto Harbor, it had more the appearance of an excursion boat rather than a machine of war. Dozens of dignitaries crowded its conning tower and deck, waving to the crowds lining the waterfront. Factory and boat whistles blasted a welcome, airplanes circled overhead, and boats of every description escorted the vessel to its berth. The *Toronto Sun* estimated that fifteen thousand people viewed UC-97 during its one-day visit.

The tour was building momentum, pushing out a wave of publicity and excitement in advance of its progress. As the submarine wrapped up its stops in Lake Ontario, the small

24. An aerial view of UC-97 in Toronto Harbor. The line of visitors waiting to tour the U-boat extends out of the picture to the right. Library and Archives Canada

community of Dunkirk, New York, on Lake Erie south of Buffalo, began to frantically pull strings to be added to the sub's itinerary. Time was getting short. The sub stopped at Hamilton, Ontario, on June 11 and departed the next day for the Welland Canal on its way to Lake Erie. Dunkirk officials phoned every congressman and naval official they could think of to make it happen. When UC-97 put in at Buffalo on June 14, Dunkirk finally got word that its efforts had been rewarded. The U-boat would stop for several hours in Dunkirk while en route to its scheduled visit in Erie.

A bugle blasting reveille and the navy call to assembly echoed through the busy streets of Buffalo. Those stopping to check out the noise got a handbill from a navy recruiter announcing that a German submarine was open for inspection at the foot of Main Street. This was not exactly news to most of the population of Buffalo. For weeks local recruit-

25. Crew members of UC-97 pose on deck during its visit to
Rochester, New York. Capt. Charles Lockwood is second from
left. Albert R. Stone Negative Collection, Rochester Museum
& Science Center, Rochester NY

ers had been spreading the word about UC-97's visit. Thousands of posters and handbills papered the surrounding
counties. Recruiters gave speeches, marched in the anti-
prohibition parade, mailed letters to prospective recruits,
and ran full-page ads in the Buffalo paper.

UC-97 was the first submarine to ever visit the city, the
Buffalo Express informed its readers on the day of the sub's
arrival. That message might have been repeated at every
city along the route, because UC-97 was the first submarine ever to sail the Great Lakes. As such, it prompted one
Buffalo paper to recall the strange occurrence in 1892 when
a Buffalo-to-Toledo-bound ship reported sighting the legendary Bessie, a fifty-foot serpent said to inhabit Lake Erie.
Bessie never eased into a berth on Buffalo's waterfront, the
paper pointed out, but on June 14 UC-97 did, a creature just
as strange and alluring as the legendary serpent.

Navy recruiters set up a table on the U-boat's deck. Young men who came on board, descended into the compact tangle of modern machinery and cramped quarters, and emerged awestruck could sign up for adventure on the spot. The navy tug that had accompanied the U-boat at the start of its voyage had now been replaced by two submarine chasers, SC 411 and SC 497, the swift wooden boats developed during the war to counter the U-boat threat. These novel vessels themselves were a big attraction. At 110 feet, they were 75 feet shorter than UC-97, but they sported impressive armament for a vessel their size, including a three-inch deck gun, a Y-gun depth charge launcher, depth charge racks on the stern, and machine guns on the bridge.

Northwestern New York was fertile recruiting territory. Since the end of the war, only New York City and Boston had produced more recruits than Buffalo. Now, with the publicity generated by the arrival of an enemy submarine in port, recruitment numbers could soar to record levels—if recruiters did their job right. The "Recruiter's Bulletin" explained it this way: "Advertising for recruits is but shaking the plum tree, the recruiter has got to go out and pick the fruit."

During the war, the navy "picked fruit" with appeals to patriotism and the moral cause of combating a villainous enemy. Men enlisted to save civilization from the blood-thirsty Huns or to redress the outrage of U-boats sinking passenger liners and hospital ships. U-boat attacks along the East Coast had spurred record enlistments in 1918. But the postwar departure of many sailors had thinned navy ranks considerably, so the push was on to redouble recruitment efforts.

With the war now over, recruitment methods had to change. The "Recruiter's Bulletin" informed recruiting officers that young men now enlisted to educate themselves, travel, or make a career. In the past, some tall promises had been made about such opportunities in the navy, but now they might more reasonably happen. The war had lifted the United States from its tradition of isolation to extend its presence across the globe. A new recruit could reasonably expect to visit South America, Hawaii, or exotic Asian ports.

Whereas during the war recruitment posters had stoked outrage over the U-boat war, now they showed sailors riding elephants in India or working with heavy machinery. Recruiters told stories of enlisted men who rose to be commissioned officers. Service in the navy was now less of a patriotic gesture than an investment in self. News reports claimed that a higher caliber of man now enlisted in the navy, young men on the go, out to better themselves.

"The world is to be made over," Navy Secretary Daniels explained in the "Recruiter's Bulletin" in the summer of 1919, "and there is a new geography and a new map. The seas mean more to us than before the World War. . . . More merchant ships have been built in the last three years than in the previous thirty. . . . Seafaring is to come into its own with better opportunities and pay. . . . We are inviting young men of capacity and ambition to enlist." Daniels estimated that the navy would have to recruit two hundred thousand men in 1919 alone to man merchant ships in government service.

The New World Order

Around eleven o'clock in the morning on June 28, word reached the U.S. fleet anchored in the Hudson River that Germany had signed the Treaty of Versailles, bringing an official end to the war. The flagship flashed a wireless message with the single word "Peace." Picked up by the merchant marine fleet, the message got relayed from ship to ship, working its way far out to sea until it met up with the same announcement traveling from the other side of the Atlantic. The ringing of church bells and a salute from the big guns of the battleship *Pennsylvania* alerted residents of New York to the auspicious occasion.

Public reaction did not match the exuberance that greeted the armistice the previous November, but the treaty marked a satisfying closure to the tragic war. The countries of the world could close the book on yesterday and be hopeful about tomorrow. President Wilson found transformative potential in the treaty's provision to create a League of Nations, which would put an end to the "old and intolerable order" under which a few selfish men "could use the peoples of great empires to serve their ambition for power and dominion." Wilson believed the treaty was a "great charter for a new order of affairs."

The following day when UC-97 stopped at Detroit, the police commissioner waited at the dock to warn Captain Lockwood about a very different new order of affairs. The U-boat had planned a one-week stay in Detroit so it could play a prominent role in the city's Fourth of July celebrations. Detroit had experienced a large and unruly May Day parade, the commissioner explained to the captain, and he feared a Red demonstration might happen on Independence Day as well. He warned Lockwood to be prepared for trouble.

Lockwood was certainly aware of the May Day rallies that had turned violent in several cities. Two weeks earlier the submarine had visited Cleveland, where a massive riot erupted from their May Day parade. Mounted police and an army tank had to be brought in to restore order. The contagion of Bolshevik revolution seemed to have jumped the Atlantic with the U-boats, carried from the infected German navy yards at Kiel and Bremerhaven, where Red revolutions took control in the final days of the war. To be on the safe side, Lockwood posted armed guards on the Fourth and had the whole crew on high alert. The police commissioner showed up late on the Fourth to sound the all clear.

26. UC-97 arrived in Detroit just two days after the signing of the Treaty of Versailles brought an official end to World War I. The U-boat took part in the city's Fourth of July celebration. Walter P. Reuther Library, Wayne State University

The spirit of any protesters may have been dampened by the carefully orchestrated arrival home of Detroit's own 339th Infantry, the "Polar Bear" regiment, fresh from fighting Bolsheviks at Archangel, in the frozen wastes of Arctic Russia. Along with British, French, and Canadian troops, the unit had been shipped there two months before the armistice in an ill-conceived plan to thwart the Russian Revolution. The unit lost 215 men and accomplished nothing. With UC-97 standing by, 1,500 men from the 339th arrived by boat and paraded the streets as heroes. The town guaranteed every man a job and fifteen dollars for each month of service.

UC-97's schedule called for visits to several cities along Michigan's Lower Peninsula and then through the Sault

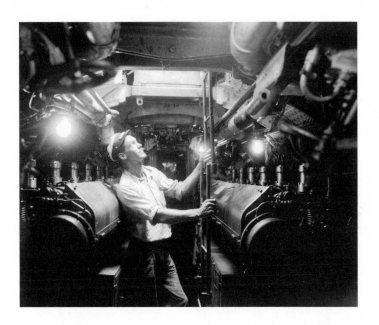

27. The engine room of UC-97. The crew struggled to keep the submarine's diesel engines functioning. At Sault Ste. Marie engine problems forced the cancellation of the Lake Superior leg of the cruise. Walter P. Reuther Library, Wayne State University

Ste. Marie canals to Lake Superior. But an all-too-familiar problem arose at Sault Ste. Marie—more burned-out pistons. The crew had been nursing UC-97's worn-out engines since they first took possession of the sub in Harwich, England. They had drilled and plugged piston heads, crossed the Atlantic with a supply of extra pistons scavenged from other U-boats, and had kept the machine shop on board their escort ship busy with makeshift repairs. Now a couple of the pistons had failed again. It was enough to make a sailor wonder about the U-boat's vaunted reputation for quality and reliability. But UC-97 was being pushed far beyond its design capabilities of short-duration missions and regular shipyard maintenance. The marathon voyage of UC-97 had stressed its diesel engines to the limit.

Makeshift repairs could keep the boat limping along, but the prospect of entering Lake Superior and sailing to Duluth—five hundred miles away—and back again, would be too great a challenge for the temperamental engines. The Navy Department refused any more expenditure for new pistons and approved Captain Lockwood's suggestion that the Lake Superior portion of the tour be canceled. A quickly improvised new itinerary would take UC-97 south into Lake Michigan, visiting as many Michigan communities as possible, and then have it support a series of navy recruitment events at Wisconsin coastal cities on the way to its final destination of Chicago.

The "Death Device of Autocratic Germany"

A former enemy vessel, especially one as novel as a submarine and as infamous as a U-boat, continued to be the centerpiece of recruitment events in the cities it visited. Sheboygan organized its Navy Day around the visit. A roadshow of entertainment came up from the Great Lakes Naval Station in Illinois—two hydroplanes, a navy band, singing quartet, baseball team, and a six-reel movie, *The Making of a Sailor.*

The movie had become a staple of navy recruiting aimed specifically at young men from inland sections of the country who had never seen salt water. They needed to be introduced to the concept of how someone became a sailor. The movie featured the experiences of a young man who enlists in the navy, receives his training, and then serves on the battleship *Pennsylvania* and plays his part in ridding the seas of U-boats and bringing about the surrender of the German fleet. It played in movie theaters in many of the cities where UC-97 stopped.

"It is particularly appropriate that the film should be shown in Wisconsin while the UC-97 is in Lake Michigan waters," suggested the *Sheboygan Press* on August 8, "as

28. The sign on UC-97 warns visitors not to touch any valves or gears as "to do so might have fatal results and might even cause the sinking of the submarine," that smoking below decks was extremely dangerous and forbidden, and, perhaps very disappointing to youngsters, "Children not allowed." Racine Heritage Museum Archival Collection.

it was the American citizen sailor-boy and his torpedo-boat destroyer which more perhaps than any other factor, put the enemy subs out of business." Any young man who wished to follow in this tradition could enlist in the navy on the deck of the U-boat, be sent immediately to the main recruiting station in Milwaukee, and be on hand to welcome UC-97 on its arrival there. "To enlist in such an honorable service as the U.S. Navy on the deck of an enemy ship, captured in a victorious war, is surely an honor to any young American!"

Crowds overflowed the waterfront during the Navy Day celebration, with long lines waiting their turn to tour the enemy submarine. Visitors entered through the rear hatch directly into the engine room, where diesel engines flanked the passageway. When submerged, the U-boat ran on electrical motors controlled from the adjacent switchboard room. The control room came next on the tour, an awe-inspiring mass of levers, wheels, gauges, valves, and indicators. From this nerve center of the vessel, the crew controlled steering, firing of torpedoes, planting of mines, and submerging of the boat. One of UC-97's two periscopes had been removed, but guests could peer through the other. It extended twelve feet above the conning tower and, when the boat was on the surface, gave the captain a range of vision of six miles.

Officers' quarters stood forward of the control room, followed by the mine-laying tubes that could place their deadly cargo while the submarine was submerged, and then the forward torpedo room. Visitors climbed back on deck through the forward hatch where the recruiter's table awaited them. When things went smoothly, three hundred people per hour toured the sub. But many were left disappointed when visiting hours closed at 3:30 p.m., and for the rest of the afternoon "crowds surged about the dock where the boat was moored and elbowed their way to the front to get a glimpse of the submarine that lay on the bosom of the water like a huge sea monster." The *Sheboygan Press* guessed that there had never been an occasion in the history of Sheboygan when so many people visited the dock on a single day.

During many visits Captain Lockwood gave a public presentation about the voyage. "We are out on a cruise to educate the public about the recent submarine campaign," he would begin. "We will show why it was so easy for Germans to run the campaign and how difficult for us to stop it." Then he would discuss the types of U-boats, how boats like UC-97 laid mines, and how through new strategies and inventions the Allies finally countered the U-boat threat.

Lockwood had become a big fan of the U-boat, and given the proper audience would extol its virtues. The tops of German periscopes, for instance, had been "penciled" down to less than an inch, making them extremely difficult for lookouts to see. Periscopes on U.S. submarines were three inches wide or more at the top and frequently leaked. U-boats could dive beneath the surface in about one-fifth the time of a U.S. sub. And into their gyroscopic compasses, the Germans had installed a second gyro, meant to keep the first one on a level plane even in heavy seas. The navy had much to learn from its U-boats.

Cities along the route rivaled each other in their lavish welcome of the U-boat, in their journalistic hyperbole, and in their interpretation of the significance of the event. "The UC-97, the grey death device of autocratic Germany, has arrived in captivity," claimed the *Milwaukee Journal.* The steamer that greeted the UC-97 in the Milwaukee harbor carried a reception committee and a band. Local officials transferred to the U-boat, and while the band played "The Star-Spangled Banner," the flotilla proceeded into the mouth of the Milwaukee River. Trailing behind came dozens of tugs, sailboats, motorboats, launches, and yachts.

Crew and passengers waved enthusiastically from the deck to the densely packed crowds on buildings, streets, and bridges along the route. As soon as the U-boat docked at the foot of Mason Street, crowds gathered at the pier. It took the rigorous efforts of policemen and sailors to form people into a single line to board the vessel. A continuous procession of the curious disappeared down the aft hatch and a short while later emerged from the forward hatch, shaking their head with wonder at the mechanical complexity of the craft and its lethal capabilities.

U-boats still haunted the memories of quite a few Wisconsin veterans of the Great War. In February 1918, 350 of them had been aboard the transport *Tuscania* when it became the first American troop ship to be sunk. Torpedoed by U-boat UB-77 off the Irish coast, the ship took 230

29. The crowds came out to see UC-97 in Racine, Wisconsin.

men to their grave. In Kenosha, where UC-97 would visit in a few days, forty-five local men had been aboard *Tuscania*, and one, Art Junker, lost his life. Kenosha's Veterans of Foreign Wars post still carries his name, the Junker-Ball Post. It was a measure of the lingering impact of that event that the *Tuscania* survivors began annual meetings in 1925 and continued that tradition for over fifty years, until the few remaining men became too old and infirmed to gather.

Final Destination: Chicago

"A New Jersey sea serpent couldn't have caused much more excitement than did the German submarine UC-97 along the North Shore today," reported the *Chicago Daily News*.

UC-97 arrived in Chicago on August 16, just seventeen days after race riots in the city had claimed thirty-eight lives. Along with labor and political protests, racial unrest erupted in several cities in the tumultuous summer of 1919.

A week of arson, looting, and murder made Chicago's race riots the most violent in the nation. Residents weary of the violence were grateful for so interesting a distraction as a U-boat. They came by the thousands to see and tour the reminder of the victorious war.

Chicago had a penchant for doing things in grand fashion. Mammoth rallies and parades during the war had whipped up patriotic passions for the sale of Liberty Bonds. Exactly a year earlier, twelve trainloads of war trophies visited the city to promote bond sales, and campaign officials displayed crate loads of captured German helmets on the steps of city hall as prizes for purchasers of Liberty Bonds. But an actual U-boat was on a far grander scale. An illuminated "Welcome UC-97" sign on city hall greeted the submarine, as did thousands of visitors. Among that throng, one person had a special reason for wanting to see the submarine.

When John Rasmussen heard that a former German submarine was visiting Chicago, he closed down his boot shop and headed for its berth on Navy Pier. Rasmussen, age seventy-five, had served on the Civil War ironclad monitor *Mahopac*, the height of warship technology in the mid-nineteenth century. He wanted to compare his memories to this modern iron warship. When the bent old man with snow-white hair and beard and silver-rimmed spectacles stepped a halting foot onto UC-97, he was enthusiastically welcomed by the crew.

Like most monitors during the Civil War, *Mahopac* looked like a large turret perched on an iron raft that barely sat above the waterline. In that sense, it resembled a crude submarine. But little else of the U-boat reminded Rasmussen of his old ship. We had no such "fancy steerin' do-dinkusses" he told the crew and not so many "fancy instruments." Lt. Cdr. Lockwood conducted a personal tour for the old sailor.

The UC-97 crew had entertained thousands of visitors

over the course of this summer cruise, including many navy veterans of the war. Most old salts carried stories of their adventures. Rasmussen was no exception, only that his extended further into the past, back to the naval sieges of Forts Sumter, Moultrie, and Fisher. He regaled the crew with descriptions of life aboard the crude iron vessels of the Civil War.

Like them, he explained, his service also extended into the quiet, lazy days after the war had ended, when the *Mahopac* lay at anchor in Washington Harbor. However, one remarkable event punctuated the tedium—a glimpse of Abraham Lincoln. One day the president rode by in a buggy inspecting the fleet. That was April 14, the day Lincoln was shot. Rasmussen reckoned that he was one of the few people left alive who had seen Lincoln on the last day of his life.

On August 21, UC-97 officially closed for public display. The U-boat had played its role in the Victory Loan campaign and now also concluded its exhibition cruise, but the men who had served aboard it for the past six months had accumulated their own collection of memorable stories. The plucky crew who had rescued the submarine from the "trots" at Harwich, wrangled its rusty machinery into a semblance of operating efficiency, navigated the small boat across the stormy Atlantic, saluted the memory of the *Lusitania*, escorted the Victory Loan ship into New York Harbor, worked mechanical miracles to keep the engines functioning on the long exhibition cruise, and cheerfully displayed the popular war trophy in forty-one U.S. and Canadian cities had developed a fondness for the old boat and for each other. Only a few of them had been submariners when their adventure began, but now all could claim the title.

Now they dispersed. Some of the sailors were "duration of the war" men, who finally saw their wartime service come to an end. The remainder transferred along with their

30. One of the postcards of UC-97 created for this popular
attraction during its extended stay in Chicago.
From the author's collection

skipper, Charles Lockwood, to his new command, the submarine R-25 in Bridgeport, Connecticut. Lockwood eventually rose to the rank of vice admiral during World War
II and served as commander of submarines in the Pacific
Fleet. He championed improvements in submarines and
torpedoes and the removal of old S-class submarines from
combat service. Through his initiatives the U.S. submarine
service became a highly effective weapon against Japan,
sinking nearly half of its merchant ships and breaking the
country's shipping links to its colonies in Southeast Asia.
It was a role very much reminiscent of Germany's U-boat
blockade of England.

Dismantling a U-Boat

UC-97 withdrew from public view, parking a short way up the
Chicago River where navy personnel and salvage contractors
ushered it into the next phase of its career—dismantling.
All equipment was to be stripped from the vessel and an

appropriate home found for its hull, which would be a year-long process. As contractors began to remove the engines, ordnance, and other critical equipment to be shipped off to various naval bureaus and yards, the city of Chicago expressed an interest in acquiring the U-boat for permanent display in either Grant Park or the Field Museum. It would certainly be the ultimate war trophy. While other communities might receive a piece of field artillery for public display, Chicago could host a genuine U-boat.

UC-97's radio equipment got shipped to the Great Lakes Naval Training Center and the Washington Navy Yard; engines, periscopes, pumps, and motors to the navy's Bureau of Construction and Repair; and navigational items to the Naval Observatory in Washington. Other yards and bureaus put in their requests for individual pieces of equipment. Not until spring did final word come down that the hull could not be given to Chicago. Terms of the peace conference had been clear that all ex-German vessels in the possession of the Allied Powers had to be totally destroyed.

On September 14, 1920, the local navy commander notified the Navy Department that all equipment had been removed and shipped. He awaited instructions on the final disposition of the vessel.

7

THE EPIC VOYAGE OF UB-88

"Gott mit uns." [God with us] This Hun inscription is carried
on both the forward and aft torpedo tube doors of the
German underseas craft UB-88, now tied up at pier 11.
It was the last thing that flashed across the mind of the
German operator before the torpedo was discharged
on its murderous mission.

—*San Francisco Chronicle*, September 13, 1919

As UB-88 finished its Victory Bond visit to Savannah, a telegram arrived at the Navy Department from the mayor of
Miami, requesting that the city be added to the itinerary of
the former German submarine. The submarine could not
stop at every small community along its route, so hosting
the war trophy was acknowledgement that the federal government thought a town sufficiently important to warrant
a visit. Miami felt the snub of being left off the list.

More than likely some in the Navy Department would
have had to resort to an atlas to see just exactly where Miami
was on the Florida peninsula. And if the atlas was more
than a few years old, it would have listed Miami's population at only a few thousand residents. Maritime charts
showed the depth of water in the entrance to Miami Harbor
at only nine feet, insufficient to accommodate the U-boat.
When the mayor assured the navy that the harbor channel had recently been dredged, the assistant secretary of
the navy, Franklin Roosevelt, agreed to add Miami to the
submarine's itinerary.

The number of people who came to see the U-boat at
Jacksonville, UB-88's second stop, rivaled the crowds of

Savannah, and the same held true for Miami. The visits were beginning to settle into smoothly orchestrated affairs. The mayor of each community received advance notice of the U-boat's visit and was asked to promote the event. Politicians met the boat at the pier or even harbor entrance so they could be standing on the deck as it docked, waving to the crowd as though deserving credit for delivering the vanquished enemy craft. Newspapermen toured the vessel in advance of the public so that the next edition of the paper would reveal their astonishment at the mechanical complexity of the craft: the wheels, dials, levers, electric motors, pumps, giant diesel engines, and the tangle of wires and pipes that controlled every action of the war machine and sustained its crew. No wonder that UB-88 had a bloody war record of sixteen Allied and neutral "kills."

In Miami the mayor and city officials seemed less interested in seeing a German submarine than in showing their booming city to UB-88's officers. Local businessmen took the officers on an extended automobile tour. Miami had been incorporated a mere twenty-three years earlier with three hundred people, they explained. Now the population approached thirty thousand, having increased some 500 percent in the last decade alone. The war was over. It was yesterday. But Miami was tomorrow, poised to explode as a metropolis in the postwar period.

At a banquet arranged for the crews of UB-88 and its tender *Tuscarora*, one Miami official suggested that if the officers would do their best with the "men higher up" to urge the government to spend the money to deepen Miami's harbor, the city could take advantage of its prime location to support the vast expansion of foreign trade expected in the wake of the war.

UB-88 captain J. L. Nielson had no special influence with Washington, so he stayed on script, telling the audience about the types of U-boats Germany had built during the

31. Jacksonville FL, the second stop on UB-88's exhibition
cruise. The submarine could not accommodate all of the
people wanting to get a firsthand look at a genuine U-boat.
Courtesy Don Pullum

war, including the small oceangoing boats like UB-88. UB-88 had been commissioned in January 1918, he explained, and operated out of the captured Belgian port of Zeebrugge where the British had staged a daring raid in February 1918, sinking several ships to block the port entrance. Compared to the larger U-cruisers that operated off the U.S. coast the previous year, UB-88 was a small boat, just 182 feet long, with a surface displacement of 510 tons. Its arsenal included torpedoes, an 88 mm deck gun, and explosive charges used to sink captured ships.

Nielson praised the American crew that rescued UB-88 at Harwich, made it seaworthy, and gallantly sailed it across the vast and stormy Atlantic. Of all the Allied countries that took possession of German submarines, only the United States had actually sailed its U-boats home under their own power. Other countries had towed them, and many of those U-boats had been lost in the process.

As word spread about these early stops on the cruise, the size of the crowds increased. At Key West, Tampa, and Pen-

32. The inscription on UB-88's torpedo tube doors reads *Gott Mit Uns*, "God With Us." The officer standing between the torpedo tubes is Gunner's Mate G. W. Raymond, engineer. The photo was taken by Roy L. Frank who served on UB-88. From the collection of Virginia Foote, Roy Frank's daughter, courtesy Gary Fabian

sacola lines sometimes stretched for half a mile. The crew perfected their routine for hastening visitors through the boat: Down one hatch, through the adjacent compartments, and out the other. They had been warned about souvenir hunters and so posted signs against such behavior and stationed a crewman in every compartment. The tour began in the central control room, which housed the giant gyroscopic compasses that steered the boat, the mechanisms that controlled the sounding machine for measuring depth, and the diving rudders or "flippers." Sixty-two storage batteries sat beneath the floor to power the huge electrical motors that drove the craft when submerged.

A crew member explained the working of the most interesting pieces of equipment in each section of the ship—the periscope, the diesel engines, the wireless radio, the tiny cooking area, the tubes from which the deadly torpedoes launched, the sleeping arrangement for the crew—and then mentioned some especially interesting feature in the next compartment, inviting the group to move along and see that as well.

In those first cities, people would still be standing in line when visiting hours ended at seven in the evening. Crewmen took up the wooden gangplank to the groans of the crowd. Their curiosity frustrated, would-be viewers stood on the pier and gaped instead, finding some satisfaction at merely being in the presence of such an alien vessel. Some of them, knowing the U-boat's itinerary, traveled to the next stop, to Tampa, Pensacola, or Mobile, hoping to get on board there. Visiting hours got extended to eight and then to nine. The most frequently asked questions: Did the deck gun discharge torpedoes? And, had the submarine sailed underwater from England to the United States? The answer to both was no.

Airplanes and Submarines

The day UB-88 arrived in Mobile, the U.S. Navy grabbed international headlines when one of its flying boats, NC-4, completed the first transatlantic airplane flight. These planes had been used during the war for long-range anti-submarine patrols. Now their historic achievement raised the possibility of regular continent-to-continent flights with implications for commerce and transportation of mail. But aside from shrinking the barrier of the wide Atlantic, the flight also shrank that ocean's protective nature even more than had cruiser U-boats during the war.

In the immediate postwar years, the debate about the future of these two new technologies—airplane and submarine—developed as parallel storylines, one driven by a flamboyant brigadier general war hero in the U.S. Army Air Service and the other by the British admiralty. The NC-4 flight brought into sharp focus the debate over the role of the airplane as a military weapon.

After winning fame during the war as the U.S. air combat commander, Gen. Billy Mitchell became a staunch champion of military air power. The world stood on the edge of a great aeronautical era, Mitchell would tell anyone who would listen, and therefore the Army Air Service should be its own branch of the military, independent of either the army or navy.

Mitchell's forceful, outspoken advocacy of air power and his penchant for publicity made him a celebrity, often at odds with his superiors. His insistence that airplanes would soon become more important defenders of our coastline than surface ships won him no friends in the navy.

For the navy, which measured its worth by the number of battleships and cruisers in its fleet, such a claim was akin to heresy. "Aviation is just a lot of noise," Adm. William Benson, chief of naval operations, proclaimed at the end of the war. "I cannot conceive of any use that the fleet will ever have for aircraft."

Mitchell stoked the conflict at a Congressional hearing by boasting that airplanes could sink any battleship in existence. All he wanted was the chance to have Congress watch while he conducted a test to prove it. Congress and public opinion forced the navy into arranging such a test. When the naval bombing experiment eventually took place in 1921, the first target for airplanes would be one of the surrendered U-boats.

It came as an ironic counterpoint that even as the airplane found an advocate for its military importance, the British pushed for a complete ban of all submarines. Their argument held that as long as the submarine remained a legitimate instrument of warfare, the threat existed of other nations repeating Germany's inhumane campaign of unrestricted submarine warfare. This didn't make sense to submarine supporters. For instance, how did you reconcile opposition to the use of submarines against the accepted use of mines? Mines sank more shipping during the war than had U-boats, and in a completely indiscriminate way.

The nightmare that really haunted British naval planners was the fear that submarines threatened British dominance of the world oceans. Any second- or third-rate country using inexpensive submarines along its coast could now fend off attacks by the greatest surface fleet of mighty battleships. Operating offensively, they could threaten great empires dependent on sea commerce. The only refuge from that scenario was the realization that by the end of the war, the Allies had effectively countered the submarine threat with new strategies and weapons such as the convoy system, depth charge, mine, hydrophone listening device, airplane, and submarine chaser.

Britain pursued the issue into 1921, proposing a total ban on all submarines at the First International Conference on Limitation of Naval Armaments in Washington DC. Notable for being the first disarmament conference in history, the meeting resulted in several major treaties, but the British found no support for restricting submarines.

The submarine had so thoroughly demonstrated its capabilities during the war that every nation was already racing to incorporate it more fully into its navy. The U.S. Navy had staked out its position on the matter by commencing an ambitious building program of twelve new submarines a month. The building campaign proved a perfect juncture to identify the best technology from the surrendered U-boats so that they could be incorporated into American submarines.

The only submarine issue concerning the United States in the year after the war was how to build better ones. By the summer of 1919 Lt. Cdr. Holbrook Gibson had been examining U-boats for the nearly a year. At Harwich, he inspected forty surrendered German submarines, and then joined the U.S. team that traveled to Germany to locate and evaluate the approximate 180 additional U-boats in different stages of construction or repair. Gibson later skippered one of the surrendered U-boats when he brought UC-97 across the Atlantic and took it through the Victory Loan campaign. He came away from those experiences with the firm conviction that the enemy boats were superior to U.S. submarines.

Now that the U-boats had fulfilled their bond-selling responsibilities, the navy transferred Gibson to the Philadelphia Navy Yard to put his considerable experience to work dissecting U-117. U-117 represented the latest in German U-boat technology, having been commissioned only eight months before the armistice. It was a long-range minelayer, 267 feet in length, with a sizeable surface displacement of 1,164 tons. It had operated very effectively off the U.S. coast the previous summer.

Gibson found much to admire in the German boats, but the U-117's huge 1,200-horsepower diesel engines made the deepest impression on him. They were things of beauty. For one, they were cast of steel rather than iron, as was used on U.S. subs. In fact, the Germans were doing things with steel tubing that the United States did not yet know how to do. But it was the quality of the craftsmanship that won the admiration of the engineering team that took calipers to U-117's internal parts—everything planned and exquisitely machined. Gibson had previously noted how quickly the Germans had evolved the technology of their U-boats. Throughout the war, they continued to experiment and perfect the mechanical details of their boats. It showed in these engines that had incorporated innovative solutions to numerous problems that still bedeviled U.S. submarines.

To ensure that the navy adopted those features of the German boats that had proven superior to those of U.S. subs, the navy technical bureaus distributed the U-boats' electrical motors, diesel engines, and other critical parts to numerous private contractors who worked on U.S. submarines.

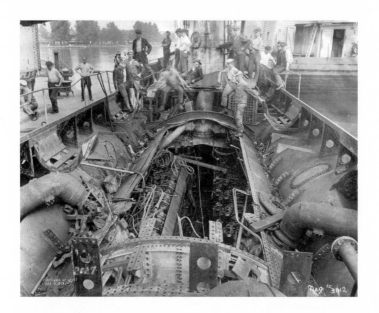

33. The U-117 being dismantled at the Philadelphia Navy Yard in 1920. Engineers adopted some of the U-boat's superior features into later generations of U.S submarines. U.S. Navy

While the navy's engineering bureaus continued to autopsy the technology of U-117, the surrendered submarines U-111 and UB-148 became the models for performance testing. U-111 underwent a series of trials to compare its performance against the latest U.S. submarine, the S-3, in diving, hull strength, torpedo firing, and maneuverability.

In these comparison tests, U-111 dramatically bested the S-3. For one, it had better armament: two deck guns to the S-3's one, and six torpedo tubes to S-3's four. U-111 had a faster surface speed and could dive in a remarkable fifty-four seconds. The S-3 submarine took a lumbering two minutes and thirty seconds to submerge. In combat conditions, the ability to quickly hide beneath the waves was a critical quality. The only areas in which the S-boat proved superior were in its higher speed while submerged, cruising range, and superior habitability.

Holbrook Gibson summarized his overall assessment of the U-boats by concluding that there were "so many things in the German submarines in design, workmanship, etc., that are so vastly superior to ours." However, he also suggested that this finding should not be made public. Rather than stimulating the rapid improvement of American submarines, he cautioned, the public release of this finding might have the opposite effect. Presumably the "opposite effect" would be that if the public or Congress realized how far the United States lagged behind the Germans, they might question the navy's ability to oversee the development of its submarines. When the findings of the U-111 and S-3 trials finally hit newspapers in September 1919, they gave the impression that while the navy could learn things from the U-boat, overall the American submarine came out on top.

U.S. submarine officers had reached a different conclusion. At the same time that many officers expressed their admiration of the German submarines, dissatisfaction with the latest American S-class submarines ran high. The navy's system of using multiple naval bureaus to oversee submarine design—and multiple ship building companies to build them—seemed to hamper its ability to match German innovation and quality. The frustration level reached such a peak that senior officers began suggesting that the United States should simply reverse engineer the surrendered U-111. Or, alternatively, the navy should go to Germany, purchase its latest submarine design, and have that be the new generation of American submarines.

Submarines on the Mississippi

When UB-88 departed New Orleans on June 7 headed up the Mississippi River, it did not have the river to itself. As the U-boat worked its way north toward St. Louis, a group of navy ships called the antisubmarine flotilla sailed south from St. Louis with its own ambitious schedule of community visits.

Conducting these two tours on the river at the same time was an inspired bit of orchestration by the navy. UB-88 put on public display the terror weapon that had threatened Britain and the Allied war effort. The flotilla, on the other hand, consisted of all of the weapons that had been used to counter the U-boats, including the U.S. submarine K-5, the destroyer *Isabel*, several submarine chasers, and flying boats and airplanes that had scouted for and attacked U-boats. A majority of the officers manning these craft had seen active service in the war zone.

Mindful of the lowering depth of the river at that time of year, the flotilla took the more prudent course of sailing directly to St. Louis, so it could work its way south. Plans were to send one of the shallow draft sub chasers and a flying boat as far north as St. Paul while another sub chaser sailed up the Ohio River to Cincinnati. The main flotilla would set a leisurely course down the Mississippi, visiting every community along the way, while staying ahead of the decreasing water level.

In the hands of an experienced river pilot, UB-88 began the month of June heading in the opposite direction, visiting Baton Rouge, Natchez, and Vicksburg, where it drew large crowds. Touring with a surrendered U-boat was not the best duty in the U.S. Navy, but not unpleasant either. Some of the American crew of UB-88 had served in the war zone, and experienced the anxiety of being stalked by U-boats or of actively hunting the stealthy killers. Matched against that, touring with the boat was a piece of cake. At times it felt like an extended vacation, but other times like the relentless schedule of a traveling circus putting on a show in one town after another.

In a post-cruise article, Captain Nielson related his

strongest impression from the Mississippi leg of the cruise. Because of the height of the levees, he explained, the crew could not see the passing countryside other than the occasional rooftop or church steeple. "On the levee the cattle graze and Negro children by the thousands, with little or no clothing, play during the hot days unmindful of mosquitoes or the torrid sun. They waved to us a greeting as we passed, then scampered down the other side to call the rest of the family."

Since the interior of the submarine became stiflingly hot and stuffy on sunny southern days, most of the crew spent as much time as possible on deck, where they might catch the occasional breeze. They rigged a sun awning over the conning tower and part of the deck to offer shade, and also netting as protection from voracious mosquitos. The crew took all meals aboard the Coast Guard ship *Tuscarora*, which served as their tender. But *Tuscarora* did not have the bunk space for UB-88's crew of thirty officers and seamen. On board the U-boat, officers had their own cramped quarters, while crew bunks were tucked tightly into the torpedo room and battery compartment.

For any resident along the Mississippi, the U-boat would have been one of the strangest craft they had ever seen on the river. It sat low in the water, like a narrow raft, but with a high-projecting conning tower. Everything about it bespoke its role as a warship. The black hull blended well against the dark waters, whereas the pale green of the superstructure made the boat more difficult to distinguish on the surface of the ocean when it searched for prey. A Maltese cross adorning the conning tower overlooked the ominous deck gun. A wireless antenna extended from the bow over the conning tower to the stern, and a sawtooth blade angled from the bow to cut through entangling submarine nets. The American crew had painted a pair of eyes on the bow to make the boat look more menacing. A wartime accident had dented the tip of the bow, but it occasionally got reported during the cruise that the damage resulted from ramming helpless lifeboats.

Since the mission of the antisubmarine flotilla was to attract the attention of young men and lure them into the navy, it courted as much attention as possible. At night, while on the river or in port, bright illumination signaled the presence of the boats. Each visit unfolded like a carefully planned military campaign. In advance of a visit, motorcycle riders posted handbills in local villages and adjacent counties. A sub chaser arrived in town days before the flotilla to make arrangements. As the flotilla converged on the town by river, the railroad delivered a navy band, glee club, and baseball team. To accommodate the full agenda of entertainment that traveled with the flotilla, some communities scheduled Navy Days during the visits and closed schools.

When U-boat and flotilla met up in Memphis in the last week of June, both had reason to be concerned about the rapidly falling river level. Making its way from Helena, Arkansas, to Memphis, UB-88 briefly got hung up on a sandbar; the flotilla had been forced to leave the destroyer *Isabel* stranded on a sandbar at Cairo. With river levels falling by a foot a day, J.L. Nielson quickly concluded that the submarine could not continue north to St. Louis and got permission from the navy to cancel that part of the cruise.

For three days in Memphis, the U-boat satisfied curious crowds who wanted to see the former enemy vessel. But never before had it been on display along with a U.S. submarine, competing with the navy's traveling recruitment carnival. In some ways they served as perfect complements to each other. Visitors could see an actual U-boat with its deadly deck gun and torpedoes that had attacked innocent merchant and passenger ships and killed women and children, and then see the vessels and equipment that had fought the U-boat scourge.

During the war seaplanes and sub chaser had worked in tandem, one locating U-boats from the air while the other rushed in to do battle. U-boats could not conceal themselves so easily beneath the surface because the chasers carried hydrophones that detected their underwater movement. Then the chaser's Y-guns would fire depth charges to destroy the submerged U-boat. The unmistakable message from the flotilla was that the United States and the Allies had vanquished this foe.

It would be left to the American submarine to offer to a handful of Memphis citizens the most memorable and frightening experience of their lives. On the day UB-88 departed for its return trip to New Orleans, five hundred curious residents of Memphis crowded onto the excursion steamer *Princess* and put out into the Mississippi. They had not set off to bid farewell to the departing ex-German submarine, but to see in action its American counterpart. At pier, U.S. Navy submarine K-5 cast off with thirty nervous passengers crowded on its narrow deck, baked by the rays of a ninety-degree sun. They were about to get a firsthand submarine experience by submerging beneath the river's murky waters.

It didn't matter to them that K-5 was obsolete technology. K-class submarines had been obsolete when the United States took them to war in 1917. Since K-boats were not meant to operate in the ocean, the navy towed eight of them to the war zone. Four of the eight boats sank on the way over, and the rest sat out the war in the Azores. Some later L-class submarines got towed across as well and conducted uneventful coastal patrols.

When K-5 reached a deep point in the river, the captain ordered passengers below. Banging knees and elbows, they descended through narrow hatches into the gloomy interior, where the temperature measured ninety-eight degrees. Hot enough to "singe the bristles on an Arkansas razorback," was how the reporter for the *The Commercial Appeal* described the oven-like interior of the sub. Hats, coats, and collars were quickly discarded.

At the flash of a light bulb, sailors twirled iron wheels hanging from the ceiling, which set off a distant roar and a vibration underfoot. Passengers mopped their brows and exchanged anxious glances. They had submerged. "How deep are we now?" a nervous passenger asked and got a quick response, "About twelve inches," which made everyone laugh. Moments later, an officer called out, "Twenty feet under," and all eyes shifted to the depth gauge. Its little needle quivered lower until stopping at twenty-four feet. There the submarine paused momentarily, suspended in the Mississippi between the surface and the bottom.

Then suddenly the nose of K-5 tipped upward, hitting thirty degrees. Everyone clutched for something to hold onto to keep from being swept into the stern. Machinery clicked, a red light bulb cast an eerie glow, and crew members spun the wheels in the opposite direction. A mere ten minutes after first submerging, the nose of the submarine popped from the water. Thirty sweat-soaked passengers emerged onto the deck into the cooling river breeze and accepted the cheers of the passengers aboard the nearby *Princess* and the hundreds of spectators onshore.

In all, the Mississippi River recruitment cruise of the anti-submarine flotilla proved a great success. During its Memphis visit, when it shared the spotlight with UB-88, twenty young men had enlisted in the navy. The flotilla spent the Fourth of July in Greenville, and then concluded its travels with visits to Biloxi and Gulfport before returning to its starting point in Key West.

Canal Passage

UB-88 cut short its own visit to Greenville because of mechanical problems and limped into New Orleans with a pronounced knock in its starboard drive shaft. The U-boat had taken much abuse in the past three months. The sand and grit of the Mississippi took a further toll, necessitating a week in dry dock for repairs.

U-boats of the UB-class, like UB-88, were short-range vessels created to operate in coastal waters. They conducted relatively short combat cruises and then returned to base for maintenance and outfitting. Part of the navy's rationale for UB-88's exhibition cruise was to see how well such small submarines held up to a voyage of this length. Having already logged over eight thousand miles since leaving Harwich and hosted some two hundred thousand visitors, UB-88 was pushing the limits of its capabilities. When the UB-88 emerged from dry dock on July 22 to face the second half of its cruise, it was joined by a new tender, the minesweeper USS *Bittern*.

It is tempting to suggest that the J.L. Nielson picked up a few promotional tips from the operations of the antisubmarine flotilla. The UB-88's stops in Galveston and Houston rivaled any so far on the cruise for the number of visitors welcomed on board. Handbills posted on railroads and in surrounding communities drew the curious from rural areas. Over twenty-five thousand people toured the boat in both cities, and tens of thousands more came to simply see the vessel.

When it departed Galveston, Captain Nielson took a party of VIPs on deck for the cruise up the ship channel to Houston. This was the first time women were permitted to travel on the submarine. At other stops, women had often hesitated to tour the interior of the submarine because of the awkward climb through the tight hatches. Not so in Houston, where a record number of women examined the boat inside and out.

The Houston Chamber of Commerce had its own notion of the publicity value of the ex-German submarine. With

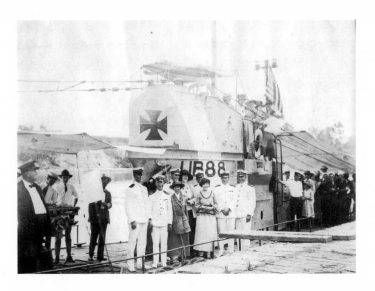

34. Women were among the passengers on board UB-88 when
it cruised the ship channel from Galveston to Houston, where
this photo was taken. To promote trade with the West Coast,
UB-88 transported a miniature bale of Texas cotton through
the Panama Canal to be delivered to actress Mary Pickford.
Photo by Frank G. Allen, courtesy Gary Fabian

news cameras flashing and movie cameras rolling, the chamber presented to Captain Nielson a miniature bale of cotton
to take through the Panama Canal to the West Coast. Like
all agricultural production, the cotton trade had boomed
during the war. In 1919 the price of cotton still stood at an
inflated thirty-five cents a pound. But demand had plum-
meted. Texas needed to find new markets for its cotton.
The miniature bale was to be taken via the Canal to Los
Angeles and there presented to movie star Mary Pickford,
who would sell it at a charity auction. This would drama-
tize how the Canal had opened the potential for Texas to
trade cotton with the West Coast and the Pacific.

Prior to the opening of the Panama Canal in 1914, there
had been virtually no shipping trade between Gulf ports

and the U.S. West Coast. But the Canal cut the distance from New Orleans to San Francisco by 8,800 miles. A month after its visit to Houston, UB-88 would fulfill its role in promoting the cotton trade when Captain Nielson handed over the cotton bale to officials in Los Angeles.

Without the Canal, UB-88 could not have made it to the West Coast. Mechanically, it could not have endured the additional 8,800 miles, and it certainly would not have survived the treacherous waters off Cape Horn. However, having the convenience of the Panama Canal did not mean it was home free.

By the route that UB-88 planned to take through the Canal, 4,500 miles separated Houston from Los Angeles. This promised to be the most grueling and dangerous leg of its journey. The crew expected the long ocean cruise to put the vessel's aging equipment to the test, and it did. About two hundred miles from the Canal Zone, damage from a tropical storm put the starboard engine out of commission. The *Bittern* had to tow the U-boat to the submarine base at Coco Solo, Canal Zone.

After repairs, UB-88 opened for public inspection at Coco Solo, at the Atlantic entrance to the Canal, and later at Balboa Heights, on the Pacific side. Many army and navy personnel and civilian employees at the Canal toured the U-boat, as did the vice president of Panama and a former president of Peru. The U-boat stopped next at Corinto, Nicaragua but departed early when cases of yellow fever were reported in the countryside. The U-boat pointed its bow north for the three-thousand-mile sail to its U.S. destination of San Diego.

First U-Boat on the West Coast

The commander of the submarine base at San Pedro, California became concerned when UB-88 did not arrive as scheduled. When the wireless station at Point Loma tried

35. UB-88 and its submarine tender *Bittern* make their way
through the Panama Canal. Courtesy Gary Fabian

repeatedly to contact the overdue submarine without success, it suspected the worst. As the days slipped by without word, newspapers reported the U-boat was feared lost.

In fact the UB-88 crew was once again up to their greasy
elbows in engine repairs, this time off the coast of Aca-
pulco, Mexico. Salt had crusted the pistons in the starboard
engine, putting it out of commission. Towing the boat the
remaining 2,100 miles to San Diego was out of the question, and Nielson wanted to avoid a long and costly port
stay to dismantle and properly clean the engine. The crew
improvised a pressure steam cleaning system that got the
engines working again, allowing the ship to finally reach
San Diego on August 29.

Although the U-boat continued to attract the curious,
the mood of the cruise changed on the West Coast. The fact
that the UB-88 arrived at San Diego three days late, after
newspapers erroneously reported it missing, contributed

to a poor turnout there. Things got worse in Los Angeles. For the first time on the cruise, the U-boat got bad publicity. A few months ago UB-88 was "a terror of the seas of which old mariners spoke in awed whispers," the *Los Angeles Times* observed. Today "its bulky sides are streaked with rust and coated with barnacles." The *Los Angeles Examiner* warned that visitors to the submarine would get their clothing smeared with grease and that overweight people would have trouble squeezing through the hatches. It didn't help that the submarine's visit coincided with a streetcar strike that limited access to the port area. Crowds at Los Angeles were the most disappointing of the whole cruise.

The further into the summer—into the postwar period—the more America's fixation on the war diminished and the more UB-88 looked like a relic rather than a trophy. It obligingly had begun to deteriorate to support that view. Its paint had faded and started to peel. Its machinery was literally falling apart.

U-boats had been built in a hurry, intended for use only for the duration of the war, and because of the wartime scarcity of copper and brass in Germany, shipyards had substituted steel, iron, and tin, which did not hold up nearly as well. Therefore, much of the piping to UB-88's main engine and the water and air lines were rapidly going to pieces. After a September 6 visit to the boat, a *Los Angeles Times* reporter confirmed that "the mass of pipes, gauges and tanks that fill the hull and excited the curiosity of sightseers during the past week are rusting out and little is left in complete working order except the engines and the periscope."

Ten cities remained on UB-88's itinerary between Los Angeles and Bremerton, Washington. Officers confessed to reporters that they doubted the boat would survive the 2,500 mile voyage to Washington and back to Los Angeles. But it did complete that journey, once again proving its durability. On its way back to San Pedro, it made an

36. ub-88 crew in San Diego. Courtesy Gary Fabian

extended stop at Union Iron Works in San Francisco, to be dry-docked and studied. It arrived back at San Pedro, California on November 8, 1919.

The gritty little boat could boast a memorable career, with a record of sixteen kills in its nine months of service with the German navy. It completed a cruise of 15,361 miles from Harwich, England to its final port at the submarine base at San Pedro, California. Over four hundred thousand visitors had walked its deck and explored its interior to gain a better understanding of the weapon that had such a huge impact on the war.

The mere presence of the ub-88 in American cities, manned by an American crew and flying the Stars and Stripes, had helped to bring closure to the raw wound suffered from the submarine war. What clearer demonstration could there be to the public that ultimately this ruthless weapon and the loathsome German strategy of unrestricted submarine warfare had failed.

In April 1920 the dismantling process began at San Pedro. UB-88's diesel engines, electrical motors, and other pieces of vital equipment were stripped from its interior and shipped off to various navy bureaus for further evaluation. This would prove to be the most important legacy of UB-88 and the other surrendered U-boats. Lessons learned from their engineering influenced subsequent generations of American submarines and contributed to the highly successful U.S. submarines used in World War II.

When UB-88 was decommissioned on November 1, 1920, all of the ex-U-boats had finished their active service to the U.S. Navy. They sat forgotten at navy yards on the East and West Coasts, and at a secluded berth in Chicago, rusting and awaiting their fate.

8

THE SINKINGS

In that part of Davy Jones's locker which lies off Los Angeles
Harbor a piratical craft which formerly belonged to
Germany is resting its evil bones.

—*Los Angeles Times*, January 27, 1921

The politicians who gathered in the Windy City in June
1920 for the Republican National Convention had reason
to be optimistic. The country was in a mood for change,
and interest ran high in whom the Republicans would pick
as their candidate, since that person would very likely be
the next president. Eight people vied for the honor, but the
spotlight quickly fell on two frontrunners: Illinois governor Frank Lowden and Maj. Gen. Leonard Wood. However,
when repeated ballots failed to select a candidate, frustrated party leaders called a recess to consider the problem behind closed doors.

One enterprising newspaper reporter from the *Ludding-
ton (MI) Daily News* took advantage of the lull in the action
to venture into the city for a "local color" story. Having
hosted nine previous Republican conventions, Chicago
anticipated the needs of delegates and reporters who wanted
to see the sights of America's second-largest city. The city's
booster club published a brochure that listed the city's top
attractions, including the University of Chicago, the house
of correction, the Chicago Municipal Tuberculosis Sanitar-
ium, and the stock yards. But this reporter instead stum-

bled upon something much more exciting in the very heart of the city—a "graveyard" of famous fighting ships.

Parked on the Chicago River, in the city's manufacturing district, sat the strangest fleet of forgotten old war vessels ever assembled on the Great Lakes. The flotilla included the *Essex*, one of the last of the navy's wooden ships that had been used to break up the slave trade on the African coast. Beside it sat the *Yantic*, built as a yacht for President Lincoln and then remodeled as a Civil War gunboat. It gained fame during the failed attempt to rescue Adolphus Greely's Arctic expedition in 1883. The *Hawk*, anchored nearby, was a former yacht commissioned into naval service to participate in the blockade of Cuba during the Spanish-American War. What a delicious time capsule of naval history this fleet represented.

Largest of the vessels in the forgotten fleet was the *Wilmette*, one of the most storied ships on the Lakes. In July 1915, under its previous name *Eastland*, this ship had boarded 2,500 excursion passengers when it suddenly rolled onto its side while still at the pier. Over eight hundred passengers lost their lives when they became trapped underwater in the interior cabins. Purchased by the navy, renamed, and outfitted as a gun boat, the *Wilmette* now served in the Great Lakes Naval Reserve Fleet.

Completing the armada was a genuine relic of the Great War, the German submarine UC-97. The U-boat sat dark and low in the water, looking rather forlorn, and yet with that menacing hunk of artillery on its deck and the characteristic sawtooth blade rising off the bow, it still cast a fearful visage on the casual observer. This was the very silhouette that had stirred panic in the hearts of so many merchantmen during the war.

But it was an empty threat now. The navy had spent most of 1920 methodically stripping the vessel of its vital equipment. Engines, batteries, radio equipment, periscope, air compressors, pumps, motors, all went to various navy yards and bureaus. Future naval officers would now receive their education on machinery donated by the Imperial German government.

This reporter's observations came more than a year after UC-97 had sailed into Chicago at the conclusion of its triumphant exhibition cruise. Even though the U-boat was not listed in the brochure of famous sights, it had become a familiar fixture in the city, so much so that the city had wanted to preserve the U-boat as a permanent reminder of the Allied victory. What a wonderful addition it would have been to the list of tourist sites in the city. Ultimately, its fate had been determined by provisions of the Versailles peace treaty that stipulated the destruction of all surrendered German naval vessels must occur by July 1, 1921, by sinking in deep water, beyond the reach of any future salvage operation. The same death sentence had been passed on all of the U-boats, and plans were falling in place how each would meet its demise.

In Chicago, naval officers decided that UC-97 could provide much needed gunnery practice for naval reservists. The *Wilmette* had been used as a training vessel during the war, but its guns had never been fired. The U-boat would be towed twenty miles into the lake, to a point where it could be sunk in one hundred feet of water, and there the *Wilmette* would blast away with its four-inch guns. Until that plan could be carried out, UC-97 waited among the graveyard of famous fighting ships for the day of its destruction.

"Slaughterer of Women and Children Gets Death Sentence"

So ran the headline in the *Los Angeles Times* on December 31, 1920, over a story reporting that UB-88 would shortly be made to suffer the same fate it had meted out to sixteen

Allied ships. By the start of 1921, all of the ex-German submarines had been fully stripped of their vital equipment, and they languished at various ports like famous guests who had overstayed their visit, the shock of their collective crimes slowly slipping from public awareness.

UB-88's time came due in the first week of January 1921. The destroyer *Wickes* sailed up from San Diego on January 2, with Cdr. William "Bull" Halsey in command. He had commanded destroyers during the war, adding to a distinguished career that would take him to command of the Third Fleet in the South Pacific during World War II. The formal surrender of Japan in 1945 would come aboard Halsey's flagship USS *Missouri*. But his mission on this occasion was to sink a relic of the last war.

Six miles off the San Pedro lighthouse, *Wickes* rendezvoused with the current flagship of the Pacific Fleet, the USS *New Mexico*. On board *New Mexico*, Adm. Hugh Rodman, commander and chief of the Pacific Fleet, had invited a party of dignitaries to witness the execution.

The naval tug *Pocomoke* towed UB-88 into position and parked it in the fog-shrouded target zone. From aboard *New Mexico*, the order went out to the *Wickes*, two miles away, to commence firing. Suddenly a flash appeared on the horizon, and a four-inch shell splashed the sea behind the U-boat. *Wickes* was steaming toward the U-boat at twenty knots when it unleashed its second shell, which tore a gaping hole in the bow of the submarine. A rousing cheer went up from the observers on the *New Mexico*.

Other shells splashed around the submarine, sending up huge geysers. Then one blasted the conning tower, bringing more cheers from the *New Mexico*. The U-boat took repeated hits but refused to go down. At one thousand yards, *Wickes* began firing broadsides. Smoke engulfed UB-88, and fire appeared through the shell holes. Still it stayed afloat. Foreseeing this possibility, the navy had planted twenty-five pounds of TNT aboard the submarine to be detonated if the shellfire proved ineffective. But the cable connecting the charge to the *Pocomoke* had been severed by the shellfire, so the explosive could not be discharged.

Finally the stubborn old U-boat yielded, its bow settling beneath the surface, lifting the stern straight into the air. Then it slipped from sight. On the *New Mexico*, Admiral Rodman ran the "well done" banner up the mast, and the civilian guests tossed their hats in the air, cheering along with the crew.

"I'm glad that German thing is done for," said Los Angeles mayor Meredith Snyder aboard the *New Mexico*.

"It is a great moral lesson to those who think they can terrorize the world with frightful slaughter," said Admiral Rodman. "The UB-88 has received the same death penalty that it had so ruthlessly passed upon many Allied vessels."

Four months after the sinking of UB-88, Submariners from the San Pedro submarine base gave a final nod to the enemy submarine that had berthed for so long in their midst. For the retirement of Cdr. Chauncey Shackford, the base gave a lavish dance at the Hotel Virginia in Long Beach, with four thousand invited guests. Everyone attending received a miniature submarine made of brass and bronze, struck from metal salvaged from UB-88.

Distant Rumbles on Lake Michigan

Just before noon on June 7, 1921, tremors shook the homes and rattled the window panes in Kenosha, Wisconsin, on the shores of Lake Michigan. Some people thought it was an earthquake and ran from their homes. Others suspected it to be another explosion at the Pleasant Prairie Powder Plant. In 1911 a thousand tons of blasting powder exploded at the plant, doing damage in a sixty-mile radius.

Responding to frantic calls, the police department quickly

determined that no other communities in the area had felt the tremors. Further inquiries turned up only one possible explanation: the Great Lakes Naval Reserve Fleet was doing target practice on a German U-boat far out in the lake. The reverberations came from the four-inch guns of the *Wilmette*, marking a final close to the UC-97. Even more so than the destruction of UB-88, the demise of this U-boat had the curious feel of an execution for past crimes.

During the first week of June, two hundred reservists and all of the ships in the Great Lakes reserve fleet gathered in Lake Michigan for the historic sinking. To add symbolic weight, two sailors were brought in for the occasion: Gunner's Mate J. O. Sabin, who had fired the first American shell of the war from his ship SS *Muscatine*, and Gunner's Mate A. H. Anderson, who fired the first U.S. torpedo at a German submarine during the war. They would serve on the *Wilmette*'s gun crews that opened up on the U-boat.

UC-97 could not travel under its own power, so the USS *Hawk* sailed down from Milwaukee to tow the submarine twenty miles into the lake, followed by the gunboat training ship *Wilmette* and a sub chaser escort.

A clear sky hung above a calm lake when the ships reached the designated location in late morning, and the *Wilmette* commenced firing her four-inch gun batteries at the U-boat. A few civilians had been invited to witness the proceedings from aboard the *Wilmette*. They put together a hundred-dollar purse for the gun crew that sank the vessel. Since he had initiated U.S. naval action in the war, Sabin took the first shot.

Moments later the reverberation of these guns would unsettle the citizens of Kenosha many miles away. But the *Wilmette*'s civilian passengers felt the full force of the guns in their bodies. The dramatic event made a lasting impression on the youngest person to witness the shelling, nine-year-old Willard K. Jaques. Jaques recalled the event in 1986 for naval historian James E. Wise, Jr.

> By the time we sighted the Coast Guard cutter *Hawk* with UC-97 in tow, I remember my excitement was sky high what with little sleep the night before. My father and I took position on the *Wilmette*'s fore deck . . . 30 feet from the port guns. We'd stuffed our ears with all the cotton they'd given us and stood on a coil of large rope to cushion the guns' concussion. My father stood behind me and with each shot would lift me by the elbows. The heat was intense [because] we were so close to the firing.

Eighteen rounds blasted from the *Wilmette*'s guns, and thirteen of them scored direct hits. Smoke curled from the U-boat's gaping wounds, its nose dipped beneath the surface, and then the vessel slipped from sight. A. H. Anderson earned the credit for firing home the lethal shot. The port gun crew, next to which Willard Jaques stood, scored five hits in five shots to take home forty dollars of the prize money. The other three crews divided the remaining sixty dollars.

Assigning the first and final shots of this engagement to Sabin and Anderson brought symbolic closure to America's involvement with this particular German submarine. It fell short, however, of bracketing America's involvement in the war itself, since the United States was still technically at war with Germany. The armistice of November 1918 had merely brought hostilities to an end, but the refusal of the U.S. Congress to sign the Treaty of Versailles because of its provisions for the creation of the League of Nations meant that a state of war still existed between the two countries. The final naval engagement with German U-boats and warships was about to unfold in the waters off the Virginia Capes. That occasion would also serve as the final naval engagement of the Great War.

The Bombing Tests

In the early morning of June 21 a flight of three F5L flying boats angled into the early-morning sky from the naval base at Norfolk, each carrying five men and four bombs. They pointed into the morning sun, heading out over the Atlantic to a designated location fifty miles offshore where they would find their target. Their mission was to prove a simple point advocated by the flamboyant assistant chief of the Army Air Service, Brig. Gen. William "Billy" Mitchell—that aircraft could sink warships.

Mitchell himself went aloft in his personal airplane, *Osprey,* a two-seat de Havilland DH-4B, with a long blue pennant streaming from its tail for identification. Not that anyone ever had any trouble locating the irrepressible Mitchell. As an outspoken advocate for military aviation, he made a habit of attracting attention. "We can either destroy or sink any ship in existence today," Mitchell boasted to a U. S. House Committee on Appropriations. "Give us the warships to attack, and come watch it." Mitchell's claims in the press and before Congress led to a public feud with Josephus Daniels, secretary of the navy, who pronounced that he would gladly stand on the bridge of any battleship when planes tried to attack it.

Congressmen liked the arithmetic of Mitchell's argument. Warships were expensive, and airplanes were not. If a $30,000 airplane could sink a $40 million battleship, then why build battleships? Within two days of Mitchell's appearance, Congress introduced two resolutions urging the navy to provide target warships for Mitchell's bombing experiment.

Fortunately the navy had some likely targets. The United States had acquired eleven German warships after the war—six U-boats, three destroyers, one cruiser, and the battleship *Osfriesland.* Treaty provisions required that they be

37. Gen. William "Billy" Mitchell held the controversial opinion that airplanes could sink warships. U-117 played a role in testing his theory. Library of Congress

sunk anyway, so why not put them to good use? Except for UB-88, sunk off Los Angeles, and UC-97, lying at the bottom of Lake Michigan, all the surrendered warships were directed to gather off the coast of Virginia in June of 1921 to participate in an experiment on the effectiveness of aerial bombardment.

U-111 sank on its own while being towed from the Portsmouth Navy Yard in New Hampshire, but all of the other ex-German ships gathered for the tests, including the three remaining U-boats: U-117, U-140, and UB-148. The tests would extend over four weeks, starting with the U-boats and concluding with the battleship.

The navy had used ships for target practice before, but these tests would be the most important and most spectacular that had ever been conducted. They would test how armored warships, ranging from a submarine to a battleship, could withstand attacks from the air and from naval gunfire. The tests would also demonstrate the effectiveness of various bombs against ships. The airplanes would begin by dropping the navy's 163-pound antisubmarine bomb and progress to the Army's 2,000-pounder, the heaviest bomb that could be carried by an aircraft. A board of army and navy officers would inspect the ships between attacks to record the damage done by each type of bomb.

When the three flying boats arrived at the target location around nine o'clock in the morning on June 21, the Atlantic Fleet waited to greet them. Nine battleships stood arrayed in a long arch, half encircling the U-117, which had been singled out as the lone target for the opening day of the tests. U-117 had been one of Germany's formidable, long-range mine-layers that had attacked shipping off the U.S. coast in 1918, and it had also mined U.S waterways. However, on this day it looked very much the stripped-down wreck, its rusty and battered deck riding low in the water. To avoid any mishaps by the attacking aircraft, concentric lines of red, white, and blue paint clearly identified it as the target ship.

Opposite the battleships stood a mini-armada of mine-sweepers, destroyers, sub chasers, and the transport ship *Henderson* that carried the members of the Senate and House naval and military committees and a host of newspaper reporters. Three blimps and five observation airplanes viewed the proceedings from the sky. No one wanted to miss the much-anticipated confrontation between naval and air power.

The elaborate attack plan called for the flying boats to take first crack at the U-boat. The largest air armada ever assembled in peacetime waited behind them, forty-seven army and navy aircraft armed with two hundred bombs. Groups of airplanes would follow in twenty-minute intervals. A squadron of Martin bombers was already winging its way to the target area to pick up the attack where the flying boats left off. Another group trailed them by twenty minutes, and a third was just taking off from the airfield. The rules stipulated that they could fly in any formation they chose and drop their bombs from any altitude. If all of the airplanes failed to sink the submarine—as many anticipated—the ships would attack, but be limited to ten rounds per gun. If that also failed, depth charges would be placed on board the U-boat to finish it off.

All eyes followed the three flying boats as they approached U-117 from 1,200 feet and dropped one bomb each to get the range. None of the bombs hit their target, thus momentarily reinforcing the notion that aircraft would not be able to even hit a warship, let alone sink it. The planes swung around and came in at a lower altitude to drop their remaining bombs.

The explosions threw up huge plumes of water and smoke and rattled the *Henderson*, sitting five hundred yards away. One bomb struck U-117 and nine fell in the "casualty zone," close enough that the concussive force of their underwater blasts could damage the vessel. The terrific impacts heaved U-117 from the water. Then immediately, its bow dipped under water.

Several times the submarine disappeared beneath the surface only to reappear for an instant. Finally, the conning tower slipped under the waves, and then the U-boat lifted its stern high in the air and dove straight for the bottom. Aboard the *Henderson*, observers shouted a cheer, and the refrain came back to them from the other ships. It had taken sixteen minutes for airplanes to sink a ship.

It is hard to say who was the most surprised by this turn of events. The Martin bombers, which had nearly arrived on location to launch their attack, were ordered to return to base, as were the other aircraft en route. The dozens of aircraft still back at base, awaiting their turn at the U-boat, were told to stand down—their services would not be needed.

In their own defense, naval authorities would focus on the artificial conditions of the test. In combat conditions, a submarine under attack would have quickly submerged, and a surface ship would have taken evasive maneuvers and fired anti-aircraft guns at its attackers. Besides, these tests were really meant to test bombs and gunfire against *armored* ships, not thin-skinned submarines.

U-140 and UB-148 became the designated victims on the following day. They would be tested against gunfire from a destroyer. At over three hundred feet in length and with a surface displacement over 1,900 tons, U-140 was one of the largest submarines afloat. The destroyer *Dickerson* opened up with its four-inch guns from a range of three thousand yards. Riding so low in the water, the submarine made a difficult target from that distance. To be effective, shots had to hit close to the water line. *Dickerson* fired thirty-nine shots. Then another destroyer went alongside U-140 with an official board of navy observers to assess the damage. They reported nineteen hits. The U-boat listed heavily, with its stern tipped beneath the surface. Minutes later, its nose rose into the air and the boat slipped out of sight.

Then came the turn of UB-148. At 516 tons, this small, coastal U-boat was less than a third the size of U-140. Four-inch shells from the destroyer *Sicard* immediately began finding their mark, hitting the deck and exploding away part of the conning tower. After forty shots, the board of observers again went alongside and determined there had been twenty hits, just before the sub rolled onto its side and went under.

EX-GERMAN SUBMARINE BEFORE BOMBING

THE DEATH-BLOW TO THE U-117

38. The navy carefully chronicled every step in the attack on
U-117. Although forty-seven planes, armed with two hundred
bombs, were scheduled to attack in waves, the first three
planes sank the U-boat in sixteen minutes. Courtesy of the
San Diego Air and Space Museum

One might think that with the UB-148 now resting on the floor of the Atlantic that America had finished with its U-boats. However, one year after aerial bombs and naval gunfire disposed of the last of the ex-German U-boats, the USS *Falcon*, a navy salvage ship, received the curious assignment to raise and re-sink U-111. Because it sank in only forty feet of water, it represented a navigational hazard. Plus, the provision of the treaty required that ex-German naval vessels be sunk in deep water beyond the reach of salvage operations.

When the *Falcon* anchored above the U-boat off Lynnhaven, Virginia, it expected to make quick work of the salvage. It had been permanently assigned to submarine salvage duties after completing salvage on the U.S. submarine S-5 the previous year. Plus, it knew exactly why U-111 had sunk. A naval board of inquiry had already determined that when the U-boat was being dismantled for examination, the removal of pipe had left some eighty holes in the hull. These had been sealed with wooden plugs. The navy assumed that one of these plugs had dislodged in heavy seas while the vessel was being towed, causing the submarine to take on water and sink.

It would be easy enough for *Falcon*'s divers to find that hole and seal it, allowing the submarine to be pumped out and raised to the surface. What had not been figured into the calculations, however, was the devilishly efficient work of the shipworm. Sometimes referred to more colorfully as the "termite of the sea," this small shell fish has a voracious appetite for wood. While U-111 sat on the bottom for over a year, shipworms had reduced all of the wooden plugs to sawdust.

The "simple job" of raising U-111 would instead extend over two months and require the assistance of eighteen seasoned divers to locate and seal all eighty holes. Once raised, it was secured between pontoons and towed to Norfolk Navy Yard, where it went into dry dock just long enough to strengthen the temporary plugs and prevent a reoccurrence of the first accident.

There would be no war games for U-111, no training of gun crews or naval reservists, no testing of the power of aerial bombs, no symbolic destruction of a vanquished foe, no celebratory cheering from witnesses as the one-time terror weapon sank beneath the waves. The *Falcon* towed the sorry-looking hulk some twenty-five miles off the Virginia Capes to where the ocean floor fell away cold and deep beyond a thousand feet. Explosive charges opened holes in U-111's hull, allowing the sea to rush in and claim the final victim of the U-boat war.

9

REDISCOVERING THE U-BOATS

This is the Holy Grail, as far as we're concerned.
—R. Adm. Alban Weber, in reference to finding the wreck
of UC-97, 1967

By one estimate, three thousand shipwrecks litter the floor of Lake Michigan—yachts, sailing ships, liners, steamers, barges, sidewheelers, ships crushed by ice, rammed, or lost in storms. They have been disappearing beneath Michigan's dark waters for over 250 years, largely forgotten until scuba diving became a popular sport and its practitioners began mapping their favorite wrecks. As diving equipment improved and new technologies made it easier to detect and view underwater sites, more of the wrecks emerged from history.

By 1960, forty years after the U.S. Navy sent UC-97 to the bottom of Lake Michigan, few people remembered that it had ever existed. That's when a chance remark by David Myers began the U-boat's return to public awareness. Myers worked as an accountant at Johnson Outboard Motors in Waukegan, Illinois. One of the other employees enjoyed scuba diving and often came to work with stories about diving on Lake Michigan shipwrecks. One day Myers suggested that he dive instead on a vessel with a more storied past, the World War I German submarine that had once visited Waukegan and that now lay somewhere at the bottom of the lake.

When his friend finished laughing, he said that there was no record of a German submarine in Lake Michigan and that none had ever visited Waukegan. He and other divers had done extensive research on shipwrecks in the lake. If such a vessel existed, they would definitely know about it. He challenged Myers to prove his claim.

At that point, the only place that Myers knew for certain that the German sub existed was in a memory from his childhood. When Myers was a boy, during World War II, his father mentioned to him that a World War I German submarine once visited their hometown, and that he had gone aboard. He walked the deck, descended the hatch, saw the torpedo tubes, the minelaying tubes, and the giant diesel engines. The image of his father in a German submarine made a deep impression on the youthful Myers that had stayed fresh in his memory.

However, when Myers went to the source of his information—his father—the reality of a German submarine in Lake Michigan turned as vaporous as a forgotten dream. His father did not remember anything about a German submarine. Undaunted, Myers contacted the local museum. The director had never heard of it, but told him to contact the navy at the Naval Station Great Lakes. The officer he talked to there also laughed at him. How would it have gotten to Waukegan, he asked, on a train? Myers even sent a query to the Bureau of Naval History, but drew a blank there as well.

By now, proving the existence of the U-boat had gotten a firm grip on Myers. His credibility was on the line. Each day after work, he headed for the local library to pour over microfilm of the old *Waukegan News Sun*. Surely, if the U-boat had visited Waukegan, it would have gotten newspaper coverage. He had no idea of the date, so it took many nights and Saturday mornings of searching. Finally, when he turned the microfilm to the August 13 edition of the paper, the banner headline jumped out at him: "UC-97 Arrives in Waukegan Harbor."

Now he knew that the U-boat was not a figment of his imagination, but he didn't know what had happened to it. The U-boat had been in their midst a mere forty years ago, so people who had seen the submarine still walked the earth. Myers called some old-timers in town, who told him the U-boat had been sunk shortly after its visit. Back to the library Myers went, where he soon located articles from 1921 that told of the sinking of the U-boat by the gunship *Wilmette*.

The exotic vessel was slowly emerging from the collective memory bin—a story from his childhood, fading memories from witnesses, old newspaper articles. The only people who remained unconvinced were those who had once owned the submarine—the U.S. Navy. The navy actually convened a Board of Inquiry at the Glenview Naval Air Station to get to the bottom of recent rumors about a German submarine in Lake Michigan. It was a crazy idea, one officer charged, and he accused Myers of making up the story just to get publicity. Myers gave him about ten minutes to hoist himself high on his own yardarm before he showed copies of the old newspaper articles. That did it. The navy was on board. They promised to cooperate in locating the U-boat.

Over the next fifteen years, finding UC-97 became something of a dedicated pastime for Myers. He talked to historians and naval personnel and obtained documents from the Naval Historical Center. The log of the *Wilmette*, the ship that sank UC-97, provided the approximate coordinates for where the U-boat went down. The Naval Station Great Lakes made the search for the U-boat the focus of training exercises.

The reservists, who trained one weekend a month and two weeks a year, had not gone through sonar training for several years. This would be perfect training. On repeated weekends they methodically crisscrossed the supposed location, sweeping it with their sonar, but found nothing. One navy officer speculated that deep layers of cold water might be interfering with the sonar signal or that the sub might be buried in silt. The whole thing played out as a curious reflection of the submarine battles of the Great War. The sailors who hunted them in the North Sea and the reservists searching Lake Michigan shared the same frustrations at the U-boat's elusiveness.

Although years went by without any additional efforts to locate the U-boat, Myers remained at the center of what had become an ongoing quest. One day he got a call from a nurse at the Great Lakes naval hospital, telling him that the husband of one of her patients wanted to talk with him about UC-97. It turned out the guy had been the gunnery officer on the USS *Wilmette* the day it sank UC-97. He had toured the submarine before it was towed out to be sunk and had removed a passageway light, which he gave to Myers. Myers had already conceived the idea of salvaging UC-97, restoring it, and installing it as a memorial at Naval Station Great Lakes in memory of all those who had served on the lakes. The light would serve as the physical symbol of that dream.

While that dream remained frustrated, Myers turned his energies to saving another local submarine. The World War II submarine USS *Silversides* had been docked in Chicago since the end of World War II and used to train reservists. In the 1970s, when the navy made plans to scrap it, Myers joined with other historians, the local Navy Reserve commander R. Adm. Alban Weber, and the former captain of the *Silversides*, R. Adm. Creed Burlingame to save the ship. The navy agreed to turn over the submarine, but only if some local group became active in preserving it.

Enter the Combined Great Lakes Navy Association. This group of navy veterans and concerned citizens devoted tens of thousands of hours to restoring the *Silversides*. The submarine remained in Chicago until 1987, when it moved to a permanent home at the USS *Silversides* Submarine Museum in Muskegon, Michigan.

Spurred by the success of the efforts to save *Silversides* and the coalition it had mobilized, the search for UC-97 resumed in earnest in the late 1970s. Myers joined the flight crew on one of the navy's big P-3 Orion airplanes when it flew over the suspected location. P-3s were the primary antisubmarine patrol plane at the time, designed to operate as part of "Hunter-Killer" groups. P-3s located submarines, and then destroyers rushed in to "kill" them. The planes carried radar to detect submarines on the surface, but also had a Magnetic Anomaly Detector (MAD) that could detect submarines below the surface. The plane searched for UC-97, but unfortunately, the lake was nearly two hundred feet deep at the site, well beyond MAD's limited capabilities.

Over a two year period, finding the ex-German submarine became the focus of sea and air exercises for navy reservists. The Navy Association also loaned its survey vessel *Neptune* for the search, which Myers used in 1978 to scan possible locations with sonar. With all this activity, the quest had begun to capture public attention. On three of *Neptune*'s trips, Chicago TV stations sent along reporters, eager to be on hand for the moment of discovery. But, once again, UC-97 eluded the searchers. TV coverage brought to public attention the long, methodical search for UC-97 and established the U-boat as the "Holy Grail" of Lake Michigan shipwrecks.

What with the navy continuing to use the UC-97 search for training and the restoration of *Silversides* going on, Myers turned his attention elsewhere. Reporters would occasionally revisit the story of the elusive German submarine and call Myers for an interview. Divers began to speculate that perhaps the U-boat had not sunk completely in 1921 and had drifted to a different location before finally settling to the bottom, which would mean a vastly expanded search area.

For Myers the long search came to dramatic conclusion in 1992 when he was invited to attend a meeting called by A&T Recovery, a salvage company operated by local divers Allan Olson and Taras Lyssenko. Since the late 1980s, A&T had been locating and recovering historic World War II–era aircraft from the lake. Thousands of navy pilots, including former president George H. W. Bush, learned to fly at the nearby Glenview Air Station by practicing takeoffs and landings on makeshift aircraft carriers. The inexperienced pilots sent hundreds of Avenger torpedo bombers, Dauntless dive bombers, and Wildcat fighters into the lake. A&T located and recovered them for museums.

However, on this occasion A&T announced a different discovery. They had located perhaps the most famous shipwreck on Lake Michigan, the former German submarine UC-97. They showed video from a remotely operated vehicle camera of the U-boat sitting upright. Its hatches stood open, and shell damage marked the deck. The designation "UC-97" stood out clearly on the conning tower.

Olson and Lyssenko had also been captured by the lure of this iconic wreck. They had worked sporadically on their own over four years, searching 140 square miles of the lake floor before locating the U-boat in over two hundred feet of water. For the time being they planned to keep its location secret. Ideally they hoped to raise the submarine and have it put on display somewhere. If recovered and put in a museum, UC-97 would be the only World War I submarine in existence.

Following the discovery, A&T explored its options for raising the U-boat and encountered a host of problems. Cost would be the first hurdle. A&T estimated recovery alone would run $1 to $1.5 million. Add the considerable expense of restoring and preserving the vessel, and that figure could easily double. And then there was the question of ownership.

In 1996, the Illinois Court of Claims ruled that the UC-97 belonged to the state. However, some experts disputed that ruling because UC-97 was a military vessel. Even sunk naval vessels still belong to the navy, they claimed, and the navy wouldn't likely support the raising of the U-boat unless some organization had a very good plan for preservation. Nor did any museum come forward with the money and space to commit to the U-boat.

This sort of wrangling over wrecks is not all that unusual for A&T. A lengthy process often follows the discovery of a wreck. For them, ships or WWII airplanes are never recovered until there is in place a comprehensive plan for recovery, restoration, public display, and funding.

Lyssenko has described UC-97 as a "back-burner project," and that's what it has remained for over twenty years. A&T has still not released the location of the wreck.

U-140, UB-148, U-117—The Billy Mitchell U-Boats

Diver, author, and shipwreck historian Gary Gentile refers to the three U-boats destroyed during the aerial bombing test in 1921 as the "Billy Mitchell wrecks." For over thirty years, Gentile has methodically chronicled the shipwrecks off the Atlantic coast in a series of books that capture their technical and human history and also serve as guides for scuba divers.

The Billy Mitchell wrecks first piqued Gentile's interest in the mid-1970s, when he began research on shipwrecks whose locations were unknown. However, he set aside the research when he learned that the U-boats had been sunk at depths of greater than three hundred feet to make them unreachable for salvage, as stipulated in the Versailles treaty. In those days such depths were beyond the reach of scuba divers.

In 1989, as he worked on an extensive series of books on

shipwrecks along the Atlantic coast called the Popular Dive Guide Series, the U-boats called to him again. To round out his book *The Shipwrecks of Virginia*, Gentile wanted to locate all of the German vessels sunk during the bombing experiments of 1921. The use of mixed gases for deep diving was being introduced around this time. Various combinations of oxygen, helium, and nitrogen protected divers from deadly nitrogen narcosis and made possible dives below three hundred feet.

Gentile paired up with diver Ken Clayton, and the two embarked on a four-year odyssey of maritime detective work and discovery. Ship's records from the bombing experiments provided approximate locations. Triangulating bearings and distances from these observation vessels to the target ships helped to fill out the picture. From commercial fishermen the men got valuable information about locations where fishing nets had snagged on underwater obstructions. Such nuisances are typically natural rock outcrops, but they can also be shipwrecks. Gentile and Clayton coordinated these locations with sites of known wrecks on a bathymetric chart of the area.

Then they began the long process of visiting promising sites and using a depth finder to confirm the existence of a wreck. The depth finder gave a picture of the ocean floor, including the contours of any sunken ship that lay there. The hard work began to pay off in 1990, when the pair located one of the ships sunk during the bombing experiments, the ex-German battleship *Ostfriesland*, at a depth of 380 feet. Clearly, visiting Mitchell's wrecks would take them into the emerging field of mixed-gas diving. Along with veteran diver Pete Manchee, the pair made a successful dive on the *Ostfriesland*, helping to push the envelope on extreme diving. They located and dived on two other Mitchell wrecks before turning their attention to locating the U-boats.

On June 6, 1992, Gentile and Clayton dove on a submarine, uncertain whether it was one of the U-boats or one of several American submarines known to have gone down in the area. The wreck sat in 266 feet of water. In the murky light, the pair made their way onto the deck, examined the conning tower, and made a positive ID. They had found U-140. On that date, they became the first persons in over seventy years to touch one of the surrendered U-boats.

UB-148 gave up its location two months later. According to records, it had gone down near U-140, both being sunk with gunfire. On August 17, they located and dove on the wreck, finding it at 274 feet, draped with fishing nets that had snagged on it over the years.

U-117 proved more elusive. Unlike its two companions, U-117 had been dispatched by aerial bombs. Naval records claimed that it sank at a depth of three hundred feet, and yet searches at locations at that depth yielded nothing. The following year, after repeated unsuccessful searches, they moved to other potential sites in shallower water and quickly located a wreck. Two dives on the site determined that it was in fact a submarine, but offered no conclusive proof of its identity. That determination had to wait for two years, while Gentile turned his attention to diving on a far more famous wreck from World War I. In 1994 he teamed up with diver John Chatterton to conduct a series of historic dives on the *Lusitania*.

The following year he came back to the waters off the Virginia Capes and anchored once more on that submarine wreck site. On this occasion he made underwater drawings of the submarine that he later compared with historic photos to make the identification certain. The vintage U-boat was not where it was supposed to be, but U-117, the last of the Mitchell U-boats, had finally been located.

The wrecks of the three U-boats sunk in the bombing experiments are now popular destinations for highly experienced divers able to use mixed gases.

UB-88—Finding the Only U-Boat on the West Coast

The former German submarine UB-88 eluded detection the longest. The U-boat first came to the attention of sport fisherman Gary Fabian in 2002 while reading about shipwrecks in the fishing grounds off Long Beach, California. First, he was amazed that an actual German submarine existed in local waters, and second, that no one had ever found it. In the way that unsolved mysteries have of transforming into obsessions, the idea of locating this illustrious submarine took firm hold of Fabian.

Because of their importance to the profession, fishermen maintain a subculture of shipwrecks, steeped in the lore of history, experience, competition, and secrecy. Wrecks are both hazards to be avoided and perfect habitats for fish. Many unknown shipwrecks were first located by commercial fishermen when they tangled their gear in them. Since this was very costly, they kept careful records of their "hangs" to avoid them in the future. These valuable lists eventually get sold, stolen, passed on, or otherwise end up in the hands of charter boat captains, recreational fishermen, and divers.

But "hangs" are often natural obstructions, and hang lists often gave only rough coordinates. Pinpointing and identifying sites was a time-consuming business, made easier in the late 1980s by sophisticated and inexpensive electronic "fish finders." Fish finders operate like sonar by bouncing sound pulses off objects underwater, such as schools of fish, debris, or the bottom of a body of water. The availability of GPS units in the 1990s allowed the recording of precise coordinates of such locations.

This was precisely the sophisticated technology that Fabian planned to employ to succeed where others had failed in locating UB-88. He had experience creating his own fishing maps and was also aware of a recently completed

U.S. Geological Survey underwater mapping project that produced high-resolution 3D images of the seafloor. Using these two resources, and working on weekends, he set on a quest to locate this missing piece of World War I history.

Log books from the navy ships that sank UB-88 gave Fabian a general search area. The U-boat went down about six miles off the San Pedro lighthouse. Geologic survey maps identified anomalies in his search zone. One by one, Fabian visited each site and inspected it with his fish-finding sonar. Most were merely piles of rocks. Any target that looked promising, he examined with a drop camera.

Fabian eventually hooked up with veteran diver and dive boat operator Ray Arntz, who had located thousands of wrecks in local waters and who also happened to be looking for the elusive submarine. In July 9, 2003, Fabian visited a promising site, about the fiftieth he had inspected, and lowered his underwater camera for a closer look. It was a shipwreck. As the camera scanned various features of the wreck, projecting the murky images back to Fabian in the boat, it came upon two gaping openings in the hull. Fabian's eyes widened, and his heart skipped a beat. They were shell holes. UB-88 had been sunk by shellfire from a four-inch gun.

On a return visit to the site with Arntz, the pair became more certain of their find. Sonar measured the target at about 175 feet in length. The UB-88 was 182 feet. The wreck appeared to be largely intact, and the few clear images from the camera bore a resemblance to the design of a UB-type submarine. The only thing lacking now was up-close video of the wreck that indisputably identified it as the long-lost U-boat.

Because the wreck lay well below the 130 foot depth considered the safe limit for ordinary scuba divers, filming would require the work of experienced technical divers breathing helium and diminished oxygen and nitrogen.

On August 27, Fabian and Arntz sent down technical divers Kendall Raine and John Walker with a film camera. Their halcyon camera lights illuminated a wreck carpeted with brilliant orange and strawberry anemones and partially draped with an old fishing net. But slowly the irrefutable features emerged—Diving planes found only on submarines; torpedo tubes; a conning tower with a steel railing unique to Type UB boats; a missing propeller and propeller shaft, both of which had been removed prior to the sinking of UB-88; and two shell holes from the four-inch gun of the USS *Wickes*. They had found the West Coast U-boat.

Even after finding UB-88, Fabian couldn't shake his obsession with the U-boat. He created a web site—ub88.org—to tell its story, and over the years has located numerous photographs and documents, and made contact with a few descendants of the American sailors who served on the vessel. The satisfaction of uncovering this piece of nautical history motivated Fabian and his team to locate and document other sunken ships and airplanes off the California coast. Their stories can also be found at ub88.org.

U-111—Salvage and Sink

Of all the surrendered U-boats, only U-111 remains undiscovered. All of its sister submarines had been a year on the bottom by the time U-111 was refloated from its shallow grave by the salvage tug *Falcon*. It spent just enough time in dry dock at the Norfolk Navy Yard to make it sufficiently seaworthy to be towed into deep water. Explosive charges sent it to the bottom 1,500 feet below, putting it permanently out of reach of salvage as required by the treaty, and well beyond all but the most determined and expensive effort to locate it.

EPILOGUE

*What manner of men were these chaps who in wartime won
the hatred and bitter execration of half of the world? Pirates,
they were called, and hanging was the destiny considered just
for them. At the same time it was perfectly clear that they
were true stalwarts of the race of adventurers.*

—Lowell Thomas, *Raiders of the Deep*

In the postwar years, the British government pressed hard
to hold German naval leaders and U-boat commanders cul-
pable for employing unrestricted submarine warfare against
noncombatant ships. The notion of holding individuals
legally accountable for violations of international law during war was something of a novelty at the time. Although
the Hague Conventions of 1899 and 1907 had codified the
concept, no one had ever been prosecuted for such crimes
under those provisions.

The Treaty of Versailles provided for such trials, but left
the details to be worked out between Germany and the
Allied governments. The Allies initially submitted a list of
nine hundred individuals charged with war crimes. The
British included on the list the names of some U-boat commanders as well as German naval leaders Gr. Adm. Alfred
von Tirpitz and Adm. Reinhard Scheer for having ordered
the use of unrestricted submarine warfare.

After considerable diplomatic wrangling, the trials commenced in a German court in Leipzig on May 23, 1921,
nearly two and a half years after the signing of the treaty.
The Allies had settled on a test list of forty-five names for

this prosecution. Prominent on the list were two U-boat commanders who seemed the most egregious violators of the rules of war for having sunk hospital ships—Karl Neumann, captain of UC-67, who sank the *Dover Castle* and Helmut Patzig, captain of U-86, infamous for sinking the *Llandovery Castle* and killing the survivors.

On trial Neumann confessed to sinking the *Dover Castle*. However, unlike Patzig, he had committed no crimes attempting to cover his actions. Only six people had died in the initial torpedo strike, and then Neumann had given time for the evacuation of all survivors before finishing off the boat with a second torpedo. Neumann freely admitted that he had been aware that it was a hospital ship and aware also of the Hague Convention rules forbidding such attacks. He explained that he had merely been following orders from his superiors. He considered those orders to be reasonable because the German government believed that the British had previously misused hospital ships to carry war supplies and soldiers. He was exonerated.

As for Patzig, the Germans claimed that he had fled the country. Two of his junior officers were tried instead. Found guilty for their conduct during the *Llandovery Castle* attack, they drew sentences of four years. However, they escaped before serving time and were later exonerated. The leniency of the German court frustrated the Allies, but the trials helped to establish the concept of accountability for an individual's conduct during war.

On July 2, as the Leipzig trials sputtered to their unsatisfactory conclusion, American involvement in the Great War came to an official end in the parlor of a country house in Raritan, New Jersey. The end had been long delayed because Congress refused to agree to the terms of the Treaty of Versailles that required acceptance of the League of Nations. The League faced insurmountable opposition in the Congress because it dictated collective action on international problems, which some saw as a surrender of U.S. sovereignty.

To officially end the state of war that still existed between the United States and Germany, newly elected President Warren Harding asked Congress to draft a resolution that would sidestep the treaty and simply declare that the war was over. When Congress finally passed the Knox-Porter resolution, it was messengered to Harding, who was visiting the home of New Jersey senator Joseph Frelinghuysen. The President returned from a round of golf, sat down in the senator's home library, and signed the resolution.

In the end, the United States ended its involvement in the Great War not with any grand treaty, but simply by revoking its original declaration of a state of war with Germany. The *New York Times* reporter in attendance was struck by the informality of the event. "More ceremony has been connected with the making of an entry in the family bible or a debutante's memory book than that accompanying the signature that ended a war that called to the colors 4,800,000 young Americans."

Although the war had ended, the United States still pursued President Wilson's pledge to build a navy that was second to none. In fact, the victorious nations were locked in a ruinously expensive naval arms race to construct the most and the largest capital ships (battleships and battle cruisers). Washington convened a naval conference in November 1921 to address the issue of disarmament. Five nations (United States, Britain, France, Italy, and Japan) agreed to limit capital ship construction; however, Britain's bold demand to totally abolish submarines found no supporters.

The 1920s proved a transitional period for U.S. submarines as the navy reconfigured how it worked with private industry in design and construction, adopted the best of U-boat design and technology, determined the optimal size of its submarines, and settled on their defensive versus offensive roles. It had long been accepted in the navy that submarines functioned best for either coastal defense or in support of the battle fleet. But the success of German U-boat tactics during the war convinced submarine officers, and eventually the navy, that American submarines should be able to operate independently on solo attack missions.

Although acknowledging the reality of an offensive role for submarines, the participants in the London naval conference of 1930 still found abhorrent Germany's use of unrestricted submarine warfare. They agreed that any future action by submarines against non-combat vessels had to follow the more civilized prize rules.

In the spring of 1919, while a fascinated public swarmed aboard the surrendered U-boats touring U.S. coastal cities, legendary journalist-adventurer Lowell Thomas began his own tour with a film lecture about the British wartime effort in Palestine. His moving pictures showed exotic scenery, veiled women, Bedouin camel cavalry, and featured the exploits of the dashing British officer T. E. Lawrence. The show proved so wildly popular that Thomas took it to London and then on a world tour. The tour established Thomas's reputation and created the larger-than-life figure of Lawrence of Arabia.

Very much the globe-trotting adventurer, Thomas returned to Europe after the war and found another figure as mythic as Lawrence, Count Felix von Luckner, Germany's "Sea Devil."

A nobleman with a colorful past, Luckner operated as a successful sea raider during the war, preying on merchant shipping in the South Atlantic and Pacific. Although Germany operated other sea raiders during the war, they had all been modern warships. Luckner had done it pirate-style in an old-fashioned sailing ship. Plus, as Thomas pointed out in his 1927 book *The Sea Devil: The Story Of Count Felix Von Luckner, The German War Raider*, Luckner had the "unique and enviable reputation of disrupting Allied shipping without ever having taken a human life or so much as drowning a ship's cat." This scrupulous adherence to the accepted strategy of prize rules in the sinking of noncombat vessels made it easy to cast Luckner as an honorable buccaneer.

While visiting postwar Germany to interview Luckner, Thomas also tracked down many U-boat officers to collect their stories. This took him into more problematic territory. Thomas had no interest in analyzing the war, justifying strategies, or explaining the impact of this revolutionary new weapon. He was out to mine the deep vein of adventure of fighting the undersea war. What these men did was by its very nature exciting, dangerous, and novel. As a frontline war correspondent and now as a reporter, Thomas wanted to glorify such exploits wherever he found them—on the hot sand of the Middle East, in a sea raider sailing ship, or beneath the waves.

Thomas's 1927 book *Raiders of the Deep* was essentially an oral history in which he allowed these submariners to tell their own stories with little interpretation or evaluation. However, since many Europeans and Americans still questioned the morality of U-boat warfare and the use of ambush attacks on noncombat ships, Thomas felt obliged to address the issue.

After the description of the actions of U-20 in the sinking of the *Lusitania*, Thomas mentions that the captain's excuse that he merely followed orders to sink any ship in those waters was not legitimate. "Civilized nations had long since established a universally recognized unwritten law," Thomas explained, that allowed them to sink noncombat ships, but only after challenging them and allowing all on board to escape in lifeboats.

With this nod to the morality of prize rules, Thomas otherwise was content to portray these men as part of the grand tradition of maritime warriors who happened to fight the war in this alien environment and in a weapon making its military debut, where they had the opportunity to define the strategy and tactics of underwater warfare. *Raiders of the Deep* helped to redefine the image of submarine warfare and the men who conducted it.

Four submarines were in Pearl Harbor on December 7, 1941, but escaped damage during the Japanese attack. At four o'clock that afternoon, orders came from Adm. Harold Stark, chief of naval operations, that all available submarines in the Pacific should immediately put to sea and conduct "unrestricted submarine warfare" against Japanese ships. U.S. submarines scored their first success nine days later when USS *Swordfish* torpedoed and sank an 8,662-ton Japanese freighter in the South China Sea.

APPENDIX

Cities Visited by the Surrendered U-Boats

The published log of UB-88 provided a detailed schedule of the cities it visited. I did not have access to the logs of the other U-boats. The dates and cities given below are largely gathered from newspaper articles. Both arrival and departure dates are given for some cities, for others only the arrival date. I encountered some conflicts and missing information. There may also have been later changes to announced schedules. In those few instances where I knew of a city visited but did not have a date, I made a reasonable guess. All dates are for the year 1919, unless otherwise noted.

U-111

April 7	Departed Harwich, England
April 19	Brooklyn Navy Yard
April 27–28	Portland ME
April 28–29	Portsmouth NH
April 30–May 3	Boston MA
May 3–4	New Bedford MA
May 4–6	Newport RI
May 6–8	Providence RI
May 8–9	New Haven CT
May 9	New London CT
June 17, 1921	Sank in shallow water on its way to participate in the bombing experiments

August 19–29, 1922	Norfolk Navy Yard, after being raised from shallow water
August 29, 1922	Sunk in deep water off the Virginia coast

U-117

April 4	Departed Harwich, England
April 11–13	Ponta Delgado, Azores
April 26	Brooklyn Navy Yard
May 2	Philadelphia PA
May 12	Baltimore MD
May 19	Wilmington NC
May 22–23	Norfolk VA
May 23–June 23	Washington DC
June 26	Arrived at Philadelphia Navy Yard
June 21, 1921	Sunk by aerial bombs during bombing experiments off the Virginia coast

U-140

May 1919	Arrived at Brooklyn Navy Yard
July 19, 1920	Arrived at Philadelphia Navy Yard
June 22, 1921	Sunk by naval gun fire during bombing experiments off the Virginia coast

U-148

April 4	Departed Harwich, England
April 11–13	Ponta Delgado, Azores
April 25	Sandy Hook NJ
April 26	Brooklyn Navy Yard
May 2	Jersey City NJ
May 2	Yonkers NY
May 2	Hastings NY
May 3	Dobbs Ferry, Tarrytown NY

May 4	Nyack, Ossining, Haverstraw, Peekskill NY
May 5	West Point, Cornwall, Newburgh NY
May 6	Poughkeepsie NY
May 7	New York City
May 8	New Rochelle, Larchmont, Mamaroneck, Rye NY
May 9	Port Chester NY; Stamford CT; South Norwalk CT
May 10	Bridgeport CT
May 11	New Haven CT
May 12	New London CT
March 10, 1920	Arrived at Philadelphia Navy Yard
June 22, 1921	Sunk by naval gun fire during bombing experiments off the Virginia coast

UB-88

April 4	Departed Harwich, England
April 11–13	Ponta Delgado, Azores
April 25–26	Sandy Hook NJ
April 26–27	Brooklyn Navy Yard
April 29–May 5	New York NY
May 8–11	Savannah GA
May 12–14	Jacksonville FL
May 16–17	Miami FL
May 18–20	Key West FL
May 21–23	Tampa FL
May 25–27	Pensacola FL
May 27–31	Mobile AL
June 1–7	New Orleans LA
June 7–9	Baton Rouge LA
June 10–12	Natchez TN
June 13–16	Vicksburg MS

June 16–18	Lake Providence LA
June 18–20	Greenville MS
June 21–23	Helena AR
June 23–26	Memphis TN
June 27–29	Greenville MS
July 1–23	New Orleans LA
July 24–27	Galveston TX
July 27–30	Houston TX
July 30	Galveston TX
August 6–12	Colon, Canal Zone
August 12–14	Balboa, Canal Zone
August 17–18	Corinto, Nicaragua
August 21–23	Acapulco, Mexico
August 24	Manzanillo, Mexico
August 29–September 1	San Diego CA
September 1–8	San Pedro CA
September 8–9	Santa Barbara CA
September 10–11	Monterey CA
September 23	Mares Island Navy Yard
September 23–29	San Francisco CA
October 1–2	Astoria OR
October 2–6	Portland OR
October 7–12	Seattle WA
October 12–16	Tacoma WA
October 16–23	Bremerton Navy Yard
October 23–27	Bellingham WA
October 30–November 6	San Francisco CA
November 7	San Pedro CA
January 3, 1921	Sunk by naval gunfire off San Pedro CA

UC-97

April 4	Departed Harwich, England
April 27	Brooklyn Navy Yard
April 29–May 14	New York NY
May 16	Halifax, Nova Scotia

May 23–26	Quebec City, Quebec
May 26–28	Montreal, Quebec
May 29	Ogdensburg NY
May 31–June 2	Clayton NY
June 2	Kingston NY
June 3	Sackets Harbor NY
June 4	Oswego NY
June 7	Charlotte NY
June 10–11	Toronto, Ontario
June 11–12	Hamilton, Ontario
June 14–17	Buffalo NY
June 17	Dunkirk NY
June 17–20	Erie PA
June 20–23	Cleveland OH
June 23–24	Sandusky OH
June 24–26	Lorain OH
June 27–29	Toledo OH
June 29	Monroe MI
June 29–July 5	Detroit MI
July 6–7	Port Huron MI
July 7	Sarnia, Ontario
July 8–9	Harbor Beach MI
July 10	Bay City MI
July 11–18	Alpena MI
July 18–21	Cheboygan MI
July 22–27	Sault Ste Marie MI
July 28–29	Mackinac Island MI
July 29–30	Manistique MI
July 30–31	Escanaba MI
July 31–August 2	Menominee MI/Marinette WI
August 2–3	Green Bay WI
August 3–5	Sturgeon Bay, Two Rivers WI
August 6	Manitowoc WI
August 7–8	Sheboygan WI

August 8–11	Milwaukee WI
August 11–12	Racine WI
August 12	Kenosha WI
August 12–16	Waukegan IL
August 16	Naval Training Center, Great Lakes IL
August 16	Chicago IL
June 7, 1921	Sunk by naval gunfire in Lake Michigan

BIBLIOGRAPHIC ESSAY

What initially drew me to the topic of America's U-boats was learning that a World War I German submarine rested at the bottom of Lake Michigan. It seemed so very far from home and so very improbably deep in the American heartland. In the way that obsessions have of taking a grip on your imagination, this U-boat and the other German submarines surrendered to the United States after the war drew me into a long investigation to discover their story.

Although many books exist about submarines in World War I, the story of the surrendered subs lay scattered in many sources. The few official accounts seemed to only touch the surface. Not until reading newspaper articles about the public display of these war trophies did I feel I had stumbled upon the real story that waited telling. I used this rich lode of eyewitness reporting as the colorful backdrop across which these U-boats sailed during neutrality, war, and the tumultuous postwar years.

1. The First U-Boats in America

There is no better source of information on the visits of *Deutschland* to America than Dwight R. Messimer's *The Merchant U-Boat: Adventures of the Deutschland 1916–1918* (Annapolis: Naval Institute Press, 1988). The *Deutschland*'s captain, Paul König, published his own account of his voyage in 1923 as *The Voyage of the Deutschland: The First Merchant Submarine* (New York: Hearst's International Library). For Adm. Albert Gleaves's recollections of the visit of U-53, see his memoir *The Admiral: The Memoirs of Albert Gleaves, Admiral, USN* (Pasadena: Hope Publishing, 1985).

To convey the public reaction to having German submarines visit a neutral America during wartime, I relied chiefly on articles from the *Washington Post, Boston Daily Globe*, and the *New York Times*.

2. They Are Here at Last

The official Navy Department report on U-boat attacks off the U.S. coast in 1918 appeared in 1920 under the title *German Submarine Activities on the Atlantic Coast of the United States and Canada* (Washington: Goverment Printing Office, 1920). Other volumes on the topic include William Clark Bell's *When the U-boats Came to America* (Boston: Little, Brown, 1929), James J. Henry's *German Subs in Yankee Waters: First World War* (New York: Gotham House, 1940), and Peter Ericson's *The Kaiser Strikes America* (Morrisville NC: Lulu Enterprises, 2008).

The *Evening Public Ledger* (Philadelphia PA) ran extensive coverage June 3–6, in the wake of "Black Sunday." James M. Merrill also wrote about public reaction in his wonderful article "Submarine Scare, 1918" (*Military Affairs* 17 [October 1953]: 181). For additional information on how the British read German naval codes to warn the United States about U-boat attacks, see Patrick Beesly's *Room 40: British Naval Intelligence, 1914–1918* (New York: Harcourt, Brace, Jovanovich, 1982).

3. Fighting the U-Boats

Edward H. Hurley's *The Bridge to France* (Philadelphia: J. B. Lippincott, 1927) tells of America's frenzied transportation of troops and war materials to the war zone in 1918. James B.

Connolly's *The U-boat Hunters* (New York: Charles Scribner's Sons, 1918) and Irvin S. Cobb's article on the sinking of the troopship *Tuscania* ("When the Sea-Wasp Stings," *Saturday Evening Post*, March 9, 1918) give eyewitness accounts of those traveling the Atlantic during what naval historian Edwyn A. Gray described as "the killing time."

Thirty-nine years after the surprise attack of U-156 at Orleans, the *Daily Boston Globe* published a detailed recap of the event in "Vivid, Blow-by-Blow Account of One of Strangest War Episodes," by Albert E. Snow, July 19, 1959.

4. Delivered into Allied Hands

See Stephen King-Hall's *A North Sea Diary: 1914–1918* (London: Newnes, n.d.) for an account of the surrender of the German U-boats. *United States Submarines* (New Haven CT: H. F. Morse Associates, 1944) by Robert Hatfield Barnes and *Building American Submarines, 1914–1940* (Washington DC, Naval Historical Center, Dept. of the Navy, 1991) by Gary Weir tell of the U.S. Navy officers who went to Harwich to select America's six U-boats. Weir's book also explains the U-boat vs. U.S. submarine debate.

Charles A. Lockwood wrote about rescuing America's U-boats at Harwich and the voyage to the United States in his autobiography *Down to the Sea in Subs* (New York: W. W. Norton, 1967), as did J. L. Nielson in "The Last Cruise of the UB-88," (*Proceedings of the United States Naval Institute* 49 [August 1923]).

5. Selling Bonds

The Story of the Liberty Loans (Washington DC, James William Bryan Press, 1919) by Labert St. Clair tells the story of America's war bond drives.

The U-boat visits to American cities played out against a backdrop of social, political, and economic upheaval. For their coverage of such topics I am indebted to: *The Last Days of Innocence: America at War, 1917–1918* (New York: Random House, 1997) by Meirion and Susie Harries; *Over Here: The First World War and American Society* (New York: Oxford University Press, 2004) by David M. Kennedy; and *The Conning of America: The Great War and American Popular Literature* (Atlanta GA: Rodopi B. V., 2001) by Patrick J. Quinn.

6. The First Submarine on the Great Lakes

For information about each of the surrendered U-boats see the navy's *Dictionary of American Naval Fighting Ships* (www .history.navy.mil/danfs/). UC-97 skipper Charles A. Lockwood devotes a chapter of his autobiography *Down to the Sea in Subs* (New York: W. W. Norton, 1967) to the Great Lakes cruise.

Other sources: *The Recruiters' Bulletin* for 1919, available through Google Books (http://books.google.com/books /about/Recruiters_bulletin.html?id=eTtHAQAAIAAJ), reveals how the U-boats assisted with navy recruitment efforts. The story of the Civil War sailor touring UC-97 appeared in the *Bismarck Daily Tribune*, November 17, 1919. The UC-97 file in the National Archives at Chicago, Illinois, includes correspondence to and from various navy offices and bureaus regarding the dismantling of the U-boat.

7. The Epic Voyage of UB-88

For more details of the UB-88 cruise, see articles by Captain J. L. Nielson, "The Last Cruise of the UB-88," (*Proceedings of the United States Naval Institute* 49 [August 1923]) and Harvey M. Beigel, "The Last Strange Cruise of UB-88" (*Warship International* 23, no. 3, Fall 1986).

Cdr. Holbrook Gibson, who oversaw much of the evaluation of the U-boats, published "The Diesel Engine of the German Submarine U-117" in the *Journal of the Society of Automotive Engineers* in July 1920. Gary E. Weir's *Building American Submarines, 1914–1940* (Washington DC, Naval Historical Center, Dept. of the Navy, 1991) is the best source of information on the U.S. evaluation of the surrendered U-boats and efforts to incorporate their technology into the next generation of American submarines. See also Eberhard Rössler's *The U-boat: The Evolution and Technical History of German Submarines* (London: Cassell, 1981). The website ub88.org is a repository of information about UB-88.

8. The Sinkings

In addition to many newspaper accounts, I consulted these articles: "The Sinking of the UC-97," by James E. Wise Jr. from *Naval History* 3, no. 1, Winter 1989; "Billy & the Dreadnoughts: How a Lone Army General Forever Altered the Face of Seapower," by John Alden Reid, in *Sea Classics* 41 (May 2008); "Billy Mitchell and the Battleships," by John T. Correll, *Air Force Magazine*, June 2008; and Alfred Wilkinson Johnson's report *The Naval Bombing Experiments Off the Virginia Capes: June and July 1921, Their Technological and Psychological Aspects*, available at the Naval History and Heritage Command (previously the Naval Historical Center).

9. Rediscovering the U-Boats

Gary Gentile's book *Shipwrecks of Virginia* (Philadelphia: G. Gentile Productions, 1992) tells about finding the U-117, U-140, and UB-148. See the website ub88.org for details about Gary Fabian's quest to locate the wreck of UB-88. I exchanged numerous emails with Fabian and also with David Myers, who spent decades trying to locate the wreck of UC-97. That wreck of UC-97 was eventually discovered by A&T Recovery, which tells of that quest on its website, atrecovery.com.

Photographs

Library of Congress: A third of the images in this book come from this source. The library has a separate Veterans History Project with photos taken by Charles Turner, who served on UB-88. Turner's daughter Sue Chapman gave permission for the use of these photos.

Leslie Jones Collection of the Boston Public Library: Leslie Jones was a photographer for the *Boston Herald-Traveler* from 1917 to 1956, amassing a collection of thirty-four thousand images that were given to the Boston Public Library. When U-boat U-111 visited Boston during the Victory Loan campaign in May 1919, Jones was there to snap a few wonderful photos. He also captured images of the *Deutschland* and U-53 when those submarines visited New England in 1916.

Albert R. Stone Negative Collection at the Rochester Museum & Science Center: Albert Stone worked as a staff photographer for the *Rochester Herald* newspaper (later the *Democrat and Chronicle*) in the early decades of the twentieth century. His work is preserved on fourteen thousand glass plate negatives housed at the Rochester Museum & Science Center, Rochester, New York. On June 7, UC-97 stopped at Rochester on the opening leg of its tour of cities on the Great Lakes. One of the photos that Stone captured during that visit appears in this book.

Wayne State University, Virtual Motor City Collection (*Detroit News*): When UC-97 visited Detroit in 1919, a photographer from the *Detroit Press* captured the occasion. Two images from that visit appear in the book.

ub88.org: This website, created by Gary Fabian, includes many photos of UB-88. Several images from Fabian's private collection appear in this book.

Orphan images: U-boats occupied such a prominent part in the war that they became pervasive in books, movies, newspapers, magazines, posters, press photographs, and so forth. Images from these sources fill the digital world and the collector's market. Such images sometimes lose all provenance. For several images used in this book, I was unable to locate the original source or the archive in which they reside.

Studies in War, Society, and the Military

Military Migration and State Formation: The British Military Community in Seventeenth-Century Sweden
Mary Elizabeth Ailes

The State at War in South Asia
Pradeep P. Barua

An American Soldier in World War I
George Browne
Edited by David L. Snead

Beneficial Bombing: The Progressive Foundations of American Air Power, 1917–1945
Mark Clodfelter

Imagining the Unimaginable: World War, Modern Art, and the Politics of Public Culture in Russia, 1914–1917
Aaron J. Cohen

The Rise of the National Guard: The Evolution of the American Militia, 1865–1920
Jerry Cooper

The Thirty Years' War and German Memory in the Nineteenth Century
Kevin Cramer

Political Indoctrination in the U.S. Army from World War II to the Vietnam War
Christopher S. DeRosa

In the Service of the Emperor: Essays on the Imperial Japanese Army
Edward J. Drea

America's U-Boats: Terror Trophies of World War I
Chris Dubbs

The Age of the Ship of the Line: The British and French Navies, 1650–1815
Jonathan R. Dull

Deterrence through Strength: British Naval Power and Foreign
Policy under Pax Britannica
Rebecca Berens Matzke

Army and Empire: British Soldiers on the American
Frontier, 1758–1775
Michael N. McConnell

Of Duty Well and Faithfully Done: A History of the
Regular Army in the Civil War
Clayton R. Newell and Charles R. Shrader
With a foreword by Edward M. Coffman

The Militarization of Culture in the Dominican Republic,
from the Captains General to General Trujillo
Valentina Peguero

Arabs at War: Military Effectiveness, 1948–1991
Kenneth M. Pollack

The Politics of Air Power: From Confrontation to
Cooperation in Army Aviation Civil-Military Relations
Rondall R. Rice

Andean Tragedy: Fighting the War of the Pacific, 1879–1884
William F. Sater

The Grand Illusion: The Prussianization of the Chilean Army
William F. Sater and Holger H. Herwig

Sex Crimes under the Wehrmacht
David Raub Snyder

In the School of War
Roger J. Spiller
Foreword by John W. Shy

The Paraguayan War, Volume 1: Causes and Early Conduct
Thomas L. Whigham

The Challenge of Change: Military Institutions and
New Realities, 1918–1941
Edited by Harold R. Winton and David R. Mets

To order or obtain more information on these or other University
of Nebraska Press titles, visit nebraskapress.unl.edu.